# *By God,*
# *You Can*
# *Do It*

# By God, You Can Do It

## A PRACTICAL GUIDE TO SUCCESSFUL LIVING

### Dr. Robert G. Kirkley

A Ballantine/Epiphany Book
Ballantine Books   New York

A Ballantine/Epiphany Book

Library of Congress Cataloging in Publication Data

Kirkley, Robert G.
   By god, you can do it.

   1. Christian life—1960-   . I. Title.
BV4501.2.K527   1985   248.4   84-24223

ISBN 0-345-32266-5

Manufactured in the United States of America
Design by Holly Johnson

First Edition: October 1985

10  9  8  7  6  5  4  3  2  1

This book is affectionately dedicated to all the loving people of Saint Mary's County, Maryland. For the last seven years, I have had the pleasure of living among them and ministering to them. Their lives are splendid examples that
BY GOD, YOU CAN DO IT.

# Contents

# Acknowledgments

*L*ike most books, this book would not have come into being without the assistance of many wonderful people.

First of all I want to thank our Wednesday morning study group in Lexington Park, Maryland, who allowed me to use them as a sounding board for each chapter. Their comments and evaluations went a long way toward shaping this book. Any writer could be helped by such support.

Secondly I wish to thank Mrs. Leila Detwiler, who had the patience to decipher my handwriting and to type the original book in its entirety through many revisions. I also wish to thank Mrs. Ann Slade, who finished the final text after Mrs. Detwiler began her vacation.

Thirdly I wish to thank the staff at Ballantine Books, whose assistance has been most appreciated.

# *Introduction*

*A*re you genuinely happy with who and what you are?

Do you feel that others less deserving than you get better opportunities and recognition?

Is the world against you?

Are you being paid what you are worth?

Are you in the wrong career?

Is your life or marriage on the rocks?

Is there any purpose to life in general or yours in particular?

You are probably reading this book because one or more of the above questions deal with sensitive areas of your life and you are looking for either an explanation or a solution and preferably both.

I must warn you that the solution to any problem in your life depends upon *you*. Many people have reached the point in their lives where they turn their problems over to others, the doctor, educator, clergyman, friends, etc., waiting for someone else to solve things for them. If we are sick, we blame the doctor. If things aren't going right at work, we blame our fellow workers or our supervisors. If there is a marital or family problem, we blame the other person and demand, "What are *you* going to do about this?"

No problem in your life will ever be solved without your directly confronting that problem. There is no magic that can change things around you until you exert your God-given powers.

This book is written to reinforce two ideas that are basic to all success:

1. *You* must be in control of your life if it is to be happy and fulfilled; and

2. God has created you and this universe with *all the power that you need* to conquer any problems, rise above any circumstance, and make your life happy and worthwhile.

It is not my purpose to increase your guilt over your circumstances, but rather to show you the secret of successful living. After your reading this book, any guilt should be gone and replaced by more worthwhile emotions.

There is a secret to successful living, and you are that secret. The following pages will reveal why and how.

# CHAPTER 1

# *Life Will Be*
# *What You*
# *Make It*

$O$ne of the great advantages given to us by modern science is the recognition of the primacy of law. Your life, whether it is happy or sad, fulfilling or empty, is a result of laws. Law governs you just as it governs all life, and one of the most basic laws of all is this concept:

LIFE WILL BE WHAT YOU MAKE IT.

Let me introduce you to some basic propositions, the truthfulness of which has been proven to me countless times by many people.

1. You have the absolute freedom to be what you want to be provided that you have clearly defined goals and are willing to pay the price to accomplish those goals.

2. Anything you want in life can be yours. You and you alone determine those goals, and no one but you can keep you from fulfilling those dreams.

*1*

3. Nothing qualitative in life is ever dictated to you or for you—not by God, the fates, cold chance, or anything else that we usually blame for our misfortunes. You and you alone determine the quality of life that you will have.

4. All limitations are self-imposed. No one outside of you can block or thwart your progress unless you consciously or unconsciously accept that limitation.

Your values or the lack of them will determine what you receive in life. Money, fame, fortune, success, power, or health can be yours. The same is true of poverty, anonymity, misfortune, failure, weakness, or illness. The choice is up to you.

You may not be aware of ever having made such choices. You may say, "I never chose to be poor" and be quite right on the face of things, but did you ever declare your intention not to be poor by actions that will enrich you? You may say, "I hate being sick all the time," but did you fail to take those measures that will guarantee your health?

Everything that you receive in life (with certain exceptions we'll discuss later) comes to you as a direct by-product of decisions you have made. There is a cause-effect relationship for everything in life. Accidents do occur, but most of the things, good or bad, that happen to us come as a result of thought processes, the origin of which we are often unaware.

It is commonly thought that God is responsible for nearly everything that happens in our world. So if lightning strikes the barn and burns it down, we say that it was the will of God. If the child is hit by a drunk driver, we say that also is the will of God. At the same time, we fail to note the contradiction of saying that such an event is the will of God, and the subsequent criminal prosecution of the drunk driver.

Such lapses in rationality are typical, however, when we seek to explain discomfort as being caused by God. It also limits our power and paints a picture of the world that isn't real. Everything that happens to you is not necessarily for your good. We live in a world where evil, sickness, poverty, and many other vices plague society. To pronounce these or other tragedies as being the will of God is to add blasphemy to tragedy.

In the play *Camelot*, when the kingdom is falling apart and King Arthur is helpless to stop it, he remarks, "There is nothing left to do but play out the game and leave the decisions to God."

But God does not make decisions for you or anyone else. God does not send suffering to you. All that God wills for you is good, but that does not rule out pain and suffering in your life. Those are decisions over which God has given you the control. You must decide for yourself the quality of your life.

We live in a world that is bounded by law. You're familiar with the law of gravity, even though you may never have studied applied physics. There are also other laws that operate in our world. Many of them, like the law of gravity, can be learned simply by observation. As an example, you cannot practice malnutrition and expect to be healthy for long. Unless you take care of your body, you should not complain when it starts to break down. Hatred, burning like a hot coal in the gut, can cause ulcers. Self-pity can cause other physical ailments. The way that you feel about yourself and others will affect how healthy you will be. You can't carry misgivings about yourself without being made ill by them sooner or later.

This gives special meaning to the words of the Bible. "As he thinketh in his heart, so is he" (Prov. 23:7). What you carry in your mind about yourself, your fellowman, the people you work with daily, your family—all will affect your ability to enjoy life.

It is high time you stop blaming God, your spouse, family members, or others with whom you have problems for the misfortunes that occur in life. You must face yourself honestly and say, "This is my life, and by God I am going to do something about it." Life will be what *you* make it.

You have the freedom and the ability to be what you want to be. You may lack the ability to pay the price. You may be undisciplined. If this is so, be honest enough to put the blame where it ought to be. The problem is you, not God. What are you now going to do about it? It is your life. Take charge of it and make it what you want it to be.

If you do not like your present circumstances, they will never change until *you* change them. No one else can change them for you. The old expression about waiting for your ship to come in is simply foolish thinking. Many people are waiting for one lucky break or for someone to come along and recognize their potential. Stop waiting for someone else to solve your problems. If your circumstances are going to change, you have to be the one to cause that change. No one can solve your problems but you. No one can help you but you. Stop making excuses and start taking action.

Life will be what you make it, and you can make it good.

By God, you can do it.

CHAPTER 2

# *Excuses We Offer for Where We Are*

When things are going well, we accept all the credit, but when they are going poorly, we place the blame on others. If we were honest with ourselves, we would accept blame for the bad times as easily as we accept the credit for the good times.

In any counseling situation it is most revealing how the counselee explains failure. "The world is against me," "Others are jealous of me," "My boss feels threatened by me," are all symptoms of an inability to adjust to adversity.

Most excuses are deep-seated and sincere, but they must be seen for what they are, namely an unwillingness or an inability to take charge of our own lives. The following are the most standard rationalizations. Since some of these excuses deal with how we view God, they are all the more insidious.

1. The first and perhaps the most widely used excuse concerns the will of God. If we fail in a project or if we are turned down for a promotion or some

other desired goal, we often say, "Well, I guess it wasn't supposed to be." Roughly translated, this means, "God didn't want me to have it."

Many people mistakenly believe that God is in charge of everything and because of that everything that happens is the will of God, whether it is good or bad. So we blame God for wars, famines, and death, as well as for the good things of life. We are so concerned about pleasing God that we become paralyzed by a fear of violating His will. This fear causes us to do nothing lest we do too much and perhaps intrude into a God-forbidden territory. Many people are kept in poverty by a fear that God doesn't want them to have too much. Others mistakenly believe that God wants them to be sickly and through suffering redeem others or themselves.

Not everything that happens to you is for your good. There is a vast difference between what happens to you and how you adjust to it. Two people may have basically the same experience in life. One of them may use the experience and come out of it a stronger person, while the other may be destroyed by the experience. The end result of that experience is not necessarily the will of God. The destroyed person should not say, "Well, this is what God wanted to have happen." A destructive reaction to a difficult situation can be the real cause of pain, not the situation itself. This has nothing to do with the will of God.

There are negative forces that surround us all. Such things as hatred, fear, jealousy, prejudice, are temporarily more powerful than the will of God. The hatred that was built into Nazi Germany turned loose in a mob was more powerful than all the sermons on love preached from dissident pulpits. Mob violence is a real thing. The civil unrest that has touched our cities makes us all realize that negativity does exert a very strong force.

When undesirable things happen to us, we should not hold God responsible. We should instead look for the real causes of the problems and deal with them rather than ignore them. When things go wrong, ask questions. Be honest with yourself even if you don't like the answers. The ability to ask the right question at the right time is a sign of maturity and responsibility. It is not irreverent.

> GOD'S WILL FOR YOU IS FOR YOU TO USE THE FREEDOM THAT HE HAS GIVEN YOU TO REALIZE ALL THE POTENTIAL THAT HE HAS PUT WITHIN YOU.

God is holding no one back. The will of God is not a confining concept. It is a liberating concept. It will liberate you from fear, failure, weakness, etc., and enable you to be the person that you truly can be.

Every person has within himself or herself far more potential than is ever realized. We often settle for something that is satisfactory when we could excel in the same thing. We do enough to get by without realizing that such an attitude denies us the thrill of being partners in excellence with God.

ALL LIMITS ARE SELF-IMPOSED.

Rather than limit us, God liberates us. "Ye shall know the truth, and the truth shall make you free." The will of God for you is a life that is full, victorious, and overflowing. Anything less than this is not from God. It may be the will of an unjust society, or it may be your own inability to overcome hangups or fear, but whatever holds you back does not come from Him.

We will explore this topic further in the next chapter.

2. Another excuse that is often used concerns the adoption of family characteristics or problems. Let a certain problem occur often enough in a family, be it physical or emotional health, or abilities, and there will be others in that family who will consciously or unconsciously adopt it. We seem to develop guilt and a feeling of disloyalty if we are different from others in the family.

Several years ago I counseled a young mother who had suspicious lumps in her breasts and was slated for surgery. In talking over the problem, she revealed that most women in her family for three or four known generations had histories of either breast surgery or death from cancer. Now it was her turn. Somewhere along the way she had started her own clock, either out of a fear of being different or the assumption that it was part of her family's medical history. After a period of intense counseling, she began to see what she was doing to herself. So drastic was the subsequent change that the surgeon canceled the operation, because the lumps disappeared.

I have counseled people who have programmed themselves for early heart attacks, mental deterioration, strokes, or other health problems simply because someone else in their family, usually a parent, has had the same problem. The same is true of failures in the work world or problems with personal relationships.

If it's been suffered in the family, it is frequently adopted by other family members.

Illness is often the escape one chooses from the traumas of life. Sometimes it is easier to be sick than well, but it is never as enjoyable.

I am not saying that there are no medically documented family problems or that one should refuse to follow a doctor's advice. I am only denying that a condition of any nature must be yours simply because someone else in the family has had it.

Such an undesirable condition is neither God's will for you nor a cross you must bear. It is your life, and you have the right to refuse secondhand problems.

Heredity can give us guidelines and warning signals, but it should never be a prison that we voluntarily enter.

3. The next excuse tells us that surrendering to weakness and suffering is a path to maturity and growth and that we undergo undesirable things in order to develop. There are many old adages such as "We are strongest when we are weak," "The way up is down," and "A man is tallest when he is on his knees." The latter one is supposedly an incentive to prayer, but I'm afraid that more often it is an excuse for begging from God rather than praising Him.

There is no lesson that you can learn from pain, deprivation, or suffering that you could not learn more enjoyably some other way. Pain is never God's messenger to comfort you. Suffering is never God's will for you.

Anything that calls for you to resign yourself to undesirable circumstances is never for your good.

This philosophy makes people stay in servitude to

situations that are hopeless. Rather than help them realize their potentials, it prevents them from being the people they could be by God.

Historically some in the Christian church have misinterpreted the role of suffering in redemption. They refer to Christ and the cross, and in the same breath they encourage us to carry our crosses. Jesus Christ did not ask for the cross. He did not martyr himself. He did not create undesirable circumstances and then claim to be persecuted for God's sake. He only did good. He helped people. The cross that was forced upon him was the making of people who could not face his honesty. The cross was their solution to their problems. It had nothing to do with Christ. But Jesus turned that cross into the greatest pulpit ever erected. Out of it came good news. This illustrates the point that what happens to you is not half as important as how you react to what happens to you.

If circumstances that are not to your benefit hold you back, turn them into something else and thereby get rid of them. Spirituality and success in life are found by overcoming your circumstances not by surrendering to them.

4. The last excuse that I want to address in this chapter concerns a concept that is quite popular at present. There are people who believe that they can do nothing about their present circumstances because this is what they have earned in life—this is their karma.

The doctrine of karma is from ancient Hinduism. It is tied to the belief that the soul makes many trips into this world through physical birth and that the level of life that one adopts in any life will determine how poorly or how well one will live in his next life.

Thus a person who mistreats others in one life will himself be mistreated in his next life. This is an over-simplification but it illustrates the basic principle of karma.

I had a conversation with a woman who assured me that certain undesirable conditions were inseparably hers in this life to pay for the misdeeds of a previous life and that not even God could remove these conditions. In other words, her condition was hopeless.

Such thinking makes people surrender to their circumstances rather than rise above them. They believe that victory is found in defeat and that worse makes better.

There are others who believe in what can be called "this-life karma," that we must pay in this life for what we have done earlier in this life. The person who abuses his body will have to suffer for that abuse later in life.

I certainly do not wish to espouse any belief that says we can disregard all consequences whatever action we take. Such a thought would be foolish.

But there are several mistakes made by both those who believe in "many-life karma" and "this-life karma."

GUILT MAY WELL BE THE GREATEST
BURDEN BORN BY OUR SOCIETY.

It seems that guilt is the occupational hazard of living in the twentieth century. Almost everyone has guilt. The rich carry guilt because so many are poor, and the poor carry guilt because they are not rich. Those who succeed in life and those who fail in life both carry guilt. Those who are healthy feel guilty about those who are ill, and those who are ill feel guilty because they imagine they are being punished. It seems that guilt as such is more related to our circumstances than to our actions. It is an adjustment problem rather than a moral problem. Guilt is an emotional crisis, and because it is a crisis, it becomes a spiritual crisis.

All guilt is self-imposed. It is the mind's way of reproving us. But often that guilt is undeserved. We mistakenly think that we have done wrong and then develop guilt, only to learn later that what we did was correct. Then the feeling of guilt disappears.

What then we are talking about is not true guilt but the *feeling* of guilt, and they are not the same thing.

The feeling of guilt is an absolutely useless commodity that no one ever need carry. Guilt does not come from God, since it is His will to remove guilt rather than to live in it.

There is an interesting side to those who believe in "many-life karma." They have succeeded in combining guilt and delusions of grandeur. The aforementioned woman was beaming when she said to me, "I am so great a sinner that not even God can help me." Any belief that so compounds problems rather than lifts them cannot be for one's good.

The first mistake that the karmist makes is not realizing that guilt is an emotional problem, self-imposed and overmagnified due to other emotional hangups.

The second mistake that they make is in not understanding the biblical concept of forgiveness. Despite most twentieth century preaching, the message of the Bible is total, complete forgiveness.

We shall discuss guilt and forgiveness in a later chapter, but I had to touch upon it now, since it is often involved in explanations used to justify our present circumstances.

• • •

12

Stop dwelling on where you are and where you have been and spend time thinking about where you would like to be.

It is self-defeating to waste time and effort explaining why we are not in different circumstances when we could use the same energy to change both ourselves and our circumstances.

Rather than offering either alibis or excuses to explain where we are in life, let us pursue getting to a better place in life.

By God, you can do it.

# CHAPTER 3

# *What Is God Like?*

*I*n the early pages of Genesis we are told that God made man in His own image. Someone has pointed out that since then, man has been returning the favor. Religion itself is always man-made. It is created to meet the needs of a given culture at a given time. That, among other reasons, is why ancient religions cannot persist. They were created for a different climate and at a different time. That is also why religions can be contradictory. Some believe in killing your enemies while another says to love your enemies. Some believe that righteous violence is rewarded by God while others believe that such violence is always wrong.

Because religions are created to meet special needs at special times, it is doubtful that we will ever see an amalgamation of all religions, for such a creation would meet the needs of no society at no time. It would be a sterile anomaly spurned by all.

It is also interesting to observe that no society can ever rise above its concept of God. This is clearly seen throughout history. Primitive people have primitive gods. Cruel people have cruel gods. Murderous people have murderous gods. Let any society become enlightened, and their concept of God will invaribly change.

Archbishop Frederick Temple in the last century introduced the phrase "the progressive revelation of God." God never changes, but people's perception of God undergoes change.

It is abundantly clear that God as revealed through ancient minds in the Old Testament is not the same as that revealed through the teachings of Jesus Christ. Jahweh, the God of the Old Testament, was seen by Israel as condoning infanticide and genocide. Whole populations, including babies, were destroyed supposedly at the order of Jahweh.

Contrast the Jahweh of the Old Testament with the Heavenly Father as taught by Jesus Christ, and you have an entirely different perception of God. The God revealed in Jesus Christ is loving, kind, and the father of all mankind. Love and forgiveness is the theme of the New Testament. This love and forgiveness, when accepted, becomes salvation.

God has not changed, but people's perception of God has changed. That explains the contrast between the Old Testament and the New Testament.

The theology, the phrases, the ideas that satisfied the spiritual needs of a previous generation are not adequate to meet the needs of a later generation. Thus the way we think about God must be constantly open to change. Inflexibility is self-defeating and unrealistic, and to some degree explains why many people leave their churches, dissatisfied by the theology or the ritual that once met their grandparents' needs. They turn to cults or other sorts of speculation.

What is God like? Several concepts must be explored and are vital to a productive spirituality. I use the term spirituality because there are many spiritual people who are turned off by theology, and sometimes a person's theology keeps him from being spiritual. I define 'spirituality' as an openness to God and all the spiritual laws that influence life.

1. The foundational concept of God is love. The God of Jesus Christ loves everybody—rich and poor, good and bad, regardless of race, nationality, sex, or other accidents of birth. Unlike human love, which is a bartering relationship, His love is always altruistic. He loves us for our good—not for His good. His love is neither earned nor conditional. He doesn't love you only if you are good or go to the right church. He loves you because you are, so He loves you as much when you are bad as when you are good. That is so unhumanlike that it gives us problems. But this is certainly the moral of such parables as "The Prodigal Son," "The Good Samaritan," "The Lost Sheep," and many more. Religion, created by man, limits the love of God to a select few, and even then it must be earned by those who must meet certain conditions. Jesus Christ rejected the narrow thinking of the religious leaders of his day, so they rejected him. It is tragic that today many Christians have espoused the theology of those who crucified Christ rather than that of Christ. As such they are more like his detractors than the master. At the very least, God is love.

2. The next most important concept of God is creativity. It is not by accident that the Genesis record

highlights creation as opposed to differing views of the time that emphasized either the eternality or the evil nature of matter.

In contrast with the Greek belief that everything material is evil and, as such, not from God, the genius of the Hebrew insight respected the beauty and holiness of all creation; about God's creation the book of Genesis repeats the theme "It is good."

The world and people in it, nature and all its beauty are but examples of God's creativity. And they are good. Your body and your mind, as creations of God, are good. Everything that God does is good.

But creation has not stopped. God's creativity is still going on. Through the pen of the writer, the skill of the surgeon, the methods of the teacher, the tools of the mechanic, and in many more ways, God is still creating new ideas in people and giving us new blessings. God is always at work, but He works through people. We have to be open to God or our progress is short-circuited.

God is creativity, and that creativity can be used in your life to solve problems and to raise you to a level of excellence. Fortunately it can be said of us all that God is not through with us yet.

3. The next most important concept of God is that He is a God of living. He lives in the present—not the past or the future.

The name Jahweh, the Old Testament name for God that was revealed to Moses, means "I AM." It literally means that God is not a has-been or a will-be. He is the God of the present; the God of the "now." People talk about the "now-generation," but since the time of Moses, the term "the now-God" has been correct.

*17*

God lives in the present, and He wants people to do the same.

*Live Now*—underline both words. That is what God wants you to do, because that is what He is doing for you and with you. Living, and not just existing, is the challenge that God offers each one of us.

God is alive, and He wants to share life with you.

Certainly much more can be said about God, but we are going to stop for now with these three concepts—love, creativity, and living. Additional concepts will surface in the following pages, but these three are the foundation upon which we will build.

Perhaps what I haven't said is glaringly obvious. I have not said that God is religious, a racist, a sexist, or some of the other connotations that we often ascribe to Him. In fact it would be ludicrous to ask what church does God attend or what religion does He practice. God is certainly not religious, He doesn't go to church, and the idea that He sits in heaven waiting for the faithful to heap praise, glory, and appreciation on Him creates an image of a God suffering a severe identity crisis and much in need of our ego-building praise. Among the many things that God is not, He is not neurotic. All theologies and other misgivings that imply otherwise must be seen for what they are, another example of man creating God in man's own image.

Among the projects that Jesus Christ undertook was the attempt to free people from unworthy concepts of God. It is a pity that we have not benefited more from the work he began.

Let us use these concepts of love, creativity, and living to free our minds from concepts unworthy of God.

By God, you can do it.

# CHAPTER 4

# *What Is God's Will for You?*

*T*his chapter is not designed to tell you whether you should be an astronaut or a mechanic. We are not dealing with specific occupations but with guidelines that will assist you as you make such decisions. These foundational concepts will influence not just career decisions but life-style, self-esteem, and many other relations that affect your life, including how you deal with others and how others deal with you.

The will of God is not a confining concept. It should never be an excuse for mediocrity. Neither should it be used to keep us in servitude. Historically religious systems have used the concept of God's will to enslave the masses, as in the caste system of India. The divine right of kings is another example of abuse. Even now many people are "kept in place" by twentieth-century adaptations of the same concept. "Woman's place is in the home," "Stay home and have babies," and similar slogans tell women that God wanted them to be secondary citizens. Others have suffered similar injustices of race, national origin, etc., and they are all traced either directly or indirectly to God.

The will of God neither confines nor denies. It liberates and entitles. Rather than suppress, it raises those who are willing to levels of living they could never reach on their own.

The theology of the mid–twentieth-century Christian has been one of denial. In the Depression period it was commonly assumed that God never wanted anyone to have very much in this life. Riches, even security, were suspect. High income was considered to be counterproductive to Christian living. Those who were poor in this world looked forward to riches in heaven. The popular preaching of the day urged people to settle for little in this life in order to have more in the next life. Thus people comforted themselves with the assumption that poverty and hunger were God's will. There are those who still believe in this unfortunate interpretation.

For them and you, here are several general guidelines we can all use to discern God's will for life.

1. Anything that keeps you in circumstances that are not conducive to growth, fulfillment, and blessing *is not God's will for you.*

2. Anything that can fulfill you or enhance your life *is God's will for you* if you are willing to pay the price.

3. God never forces His will on anyone but does place before each individual the opportunity of being something unique and wonderful.

Let's examine what these guidelines mean in life.

1. Do you feel fulfilled?

You are a unique individual. The genes and chromosomes you have inherited through your parents assure that there is no one else in the entire world exactly like you. You are a combination of talent, personality, and potential that can be utilized to do something for this world that no one else can possibly duplicate. This potential in concert with the people that you influence and who in turn influence others forms an even more unique combination.

The talents that you possess are given as a blessing to you and the world around you. God's will for your life is the utilization of those talents. Not to use them is to deny to the world something that God has designed. Talents can never be overused, though often they are wasted.

Usually talents are obvious, but sometimes they remain untapped. The easiest way to discern undiscovered talent is to ask such questions as "What would I really like to do?" Desire and talent are usually matched. What a person desires to do is usually the best indicator of what they ought to be doing.

Sometimes we are just lazy and unwilling to pay the price necessitated by the talent. Most careers require lengthy preparation or discipline. It is easier to take a job than to take the required training for the thing we really desire. If that is our problem, then we should not blame our lack of fulfillment on God.

GOD'S WILL FOR YOUR LIFE IS A
SENSE OF FULFILLMENT AND
ACCOMPLISHMENT. IF YOU FEEL
THAT YOU AND YOUR LIFE HAVE
BEEN WASTED, THEN SOMETHING IS
AMISS.

Everyone needs to feel worthwhile, useful, and necessary. Not to experience these feelings is to suffer an identity crisis. If what you are doing does not give you a sense of self-worth—don't blame God. Look around for what you should be doing and then discover how you can attain this new goal.

Maybe a career change is in order. Perhaps it will be expensive, but the sense of accomplishment will be worth the price. Maybe you don't need to change careers. Perhaps for you all that is necessary is to start doing something additional. But there is always some action you can take to insure the concept of fulfillment.

God's will for your life is the sense of self-esteem and worthwhileness without which life becomes drudgery and pain.

2. Are you happy? Are you enjoying life?

Life is too wonderful to be simply endured or tolerated. God's will is for each person to discover the spiritual laws that will generate happiness and enjoyment of living.

Boredom, discontent, and misery mark the average person in the twentieth century. That is both a fact and a tragedy.

This may be shocking to you, but God is a being of happiness. God is happy, despite what theologians have said. This is not to say that He approves of the mess that we have made of His creation. We can't be happy with that, so God certainly is not happy about it either. But the concept of a happy God is a necessary concept when you consider other options. God is certainly not morose, sullen, or gloomy. God is also not negative. That means that godlikeness necessarily includes happiness. Happiness in God is a contagious, creative sense of the enjoyment of life, and He wants all of us to share in that contagious creative enjoyment.

If your life is not bringing you happiness, then make some changes. Change yourself, change your job, change your circumstances—but change something. It is never God's will for a person to stay in circumstances that bring misery and suffering.

Happiness and fulfillment usually go together. The lack of happiness is symptomatic of other problems. Often the person feels unfulfilled or frustrated. But if what you are doing makes you unhappy, then something is wrong and to that degree that something is not God's will for you.

God wants no one to live an unhappy life. He desires that all of His creation share in the enjoyment of life.

However, someone will ask, "Isn't what I am doing so important that my happiness is immaterial?" Maybe what you are doing needs to be done, but maybe someone else ought to be doing it. In a later chapter we will address the very mistaken notion of martyrdom and self-sacrifice that has crept into Christian thought. Until we more fully examine that topic, simply accept that God has never assigned to anyone the task of living an unhappy life.

If you are unhappy in what you are doing, changes are in order, and by God you can make those changes.

3. Are you growing as a person?

Most people in twentieth century America suffer from too much training and too little education. "Training" refers to preparations for a career. Doctors, lawyers, schoolteachers, clergymen, and a host of other professionals undergo many years of it before they can move ahead in their chosen fields. But training in no way guarantees education. "Education" means being prepared for living a life that is well-rounded and full. Training is narrow while education is broad.

Learning and growing must be lifelong projects. The person who has stopped growing has started to die whether or not the physical symptoms are there.

It is to our shame that we spend far more on entertainment than we do on education. We seem to think that we have learned enough, and we now wish to be amused. The insatiable appetite for entertainment reveals how unhappy we are individually and as a nation.

If what you are doing is not leading to your individual growth, then changes are in order. It is God's will for you to be an ever-growing person, never content with past accomplishments and always eager to learn new things, adopt new ideas, and have new experiences. Too many people resign themselves to circumstances that do not lead to their growth and end up wasting precious time.

Every part of your life requires growth or it will deteriorate.

Growth is important not only for time but also for eternity. The lessons that we refuse to learn in this life may have to be learned in eternity. No one can ever learn too much. Eternity is simply the extension of time, and the learning process will continue.

Mentally, emotionally, and spiritually, we need to grow. Not to grow is to deny ourselves. It is the loss of personhood.

God has arranged for your growth. The potential is there, but you must claim it for yourself. You share creativity with God, and your creativity can only emerge through growth.

Fulfillment, happiness, and growth is God's will for

your life. If you are realizing these things in your life, then to that degree you are fulfilling God's will for you. If you have the holiest and most revered position possible and lack these things, you are not centered in God's will regardless of what you are doing.

God has made everything possible for you. You can realize these blessings and many more. Give it a try.

By God, you can do it.

# CHAPTER 5

# *God, Sin, and You*

*A*re you a sinner? Does God think you are a sinner—if so, what does it mean?

The question of sin is as old as the concept of divinity. Once man compares himself to something higher than himself, he recognizes his own weakness. This was not particularly troublesome in some ancient religious systems because their gods were not particularly moral, given to rape, murder and a host of other undesirable activities. Civilization, then and now, duplicates its concept of its gods and vice versa.

The real contrast between God and man came with the stream that produced the Judeo-Christian tradition. We do not know where it began, because it precedes recorded history, but one of the great contributions of the Hebrews was the God of morality.

Jahweh, the Hebrew God, demanded righteousness from his people, and since it was not there, a very involved sacrificial system was instituted. These sacrifices were believed to placate Jahweh's anger when the people violated his law. However, the system really made people more sin-conscious than God-conscious and thus was counterproductive.

IF ONE IS PREOCCUPIED WITH NEGATIVITY AND A SENSE OF GUILT, THERE CAN BE NO SPIRITUAL GROWTH.

What we see happening in Biblical history is still being duplicated today. Knowing God often seems an experience tantamount to a corporate relationship. Just as the ancient Hebrews believed that salvation was bestowed by joining in fellowship and observing the ritualistic worship, groups exist today who insist that salvation is dispensed only through being a member of their corporate fellowship. This is the basis for the concept of closed communion in some groups, namely that you can receive Holy Communion only if you are a member in good standing (i.e., approved by others). The fear of excommunication has been strong for violators of church laws. Not being in good community standing is the same as never being able to receive salvation in this world or eternity.

Historically it has been believed that the system, that is, the church or the denomination, conferred righteousness or 'grace'. If you had grace, then supposedly you had salvation and a potential for forgiveness even if such concepts as purgatory or suffering were also involved.

Any belief that dispenses God's grace through a corporate structure is contrary to spiritual law and spirituality itself. Spirituality depends solely upon your awareness of spiritual law and not upon your relationship with a group, a creed, or a way of life.

Sin means that we are human, and being human means that we will sin. The apostle Paul covers this very clearly in Romans 7 (in the Bible), where he describes the poignancy of being both spiritual and physical.

It is so foolish to talk about big sins or little sins. Being human is being human, and the size or quantity of our sin is totally irrelevant. Those who worry about not committing a sin so great that it would keep them from going to Heaven really do not understand the whole concept.

The biblical interpretation is that God has diagnosed every person as being a sinner in order that He might have mercy upon all. The diagnosis of sin was not for the purpose of condemning the world. God is interested in things that are positive.

In other words, the diagnosis of sin makes you eligible for God's help.

But remember that once you recognize sin as the diagnosis, it's time to get on to the cure. Some people talk about sin as though it were incurable and no one could do anything about it. If I went to a doctor with a problem and all he ever talked about was my terrible diagnosis and never discussed the cure, sooner or later I would leave that doctor to find one who was more interested in the cure. God is interested in our spiritual health not sickness.

How much have you sinned? How bad have been your sins? Are your sins big ones or little ones? None of these are important. Sin is sin.

To say that we are sinners merely means that we need God's help. No one can make it on his/her own.

Everyone needs the help that God is here to give us. That help is love.

God does not instill guilt or make us feel inferior. God is not interested in people groveling in sin. The constant emphasis upon sin is counterproductive to spirituality and only reveals people's tremendous insecurities. This message is not from God.

Likewise it is counterproductive to have people go to church week after week only to receive a repeated emphasis upon how sinful they are. People are drawn to God through love and a desire to be close with Him. In this lies the cure. Simply to emphasize sin is never enough, just as the diagnosis is unnecessary once the cure has been found.

The cross in Christianity is the symbol of forgiveness not condemnation. The Bible emphasizes forgiveness. Look closely at the ministry of Jesus Christ. Look at the people to whom he extended love:

1. The woman taken in adultery (John 8:11),
2. Zacchaeus (Luke 19:9),
3. Blind Bartimaeus (Mark 10:52),
4. The paralytic (Mark 2:5),
5. The prostitute (Luke 7:48),
6. The parable of the prodigal son (Luke 15).

Many more could be added.

The only people that Jesus ever condemned were the religious leaders who had brainwashed their followers into a sin-consciousness rather than a God-consciousness. The religious leaders condemned Christ for his emphasis upon forgiveness because they knew how powerful a faith based on forgiveness could become.

Let me summarize some of the basic thoughts of this chapter:

1. We all are human and therefore can be classified as sinners.

2. To be a sinner is simply to have a need of God.

3. God is more interested in forgiveness than in guilt.

4. Love is God's cure for sin.

5. Once you have found God's remedy, the diagnosis is irrelevant.

Instead of groveling in sin or being discouraged by your humanness, remember that God created you as a human and that is a good thing. What God has called holy, don't you then call unholy. Accept the reality of forgiveness and love that is offered to all.

By God, you can do it.

CHAPTER 6

# *You and Your Circumstances*

*M*any people believe that happiness for them depends upon changing their circumstances. They think that the answer to their problem is more money, a new job, meeting new friends, or living in a different place. This mentality is the reverse of what it should be. Your circumstances do not create you; you create your circumstances.

It is a bitter pill to swallow, but the truth is that we do create the circumstances that surround us. Sometimes the action is deliberate and visible, but often it is a result of omission—the things that we fail to do.

Let me share with you a secret of successful living.

WHEN YOU FIND YOURSELF IN
CIRCUMSTANCES NOT TO YOUR
LIKING, DON'T TRY TO CHANGE
THE CIRCUMSTANCES. CHANGE
YOURSELF, AND THEN YOUR
CIRCUMSTANCES WILL CHANGE.

Before we study this secret further, let me make it clear that I am not referring to such circumstances as accidents caused by others or to the victims of crimes. Those are circumstances that invade the privacy of others, not circumstances we create for ourselves. The circumstances I have in mind are those that the individual is responsible for; either wholly or in part. The line that divides these two kinds of circumstances is quite clear. If no one else is involved, then the probability is very high that the responsibility lies at your door.

Then there is the issue of partial responsibility. Family relationships pose problems that are a good example of this. Parents do not always deserve the way their children treat them. The relationships of husbands and wives are not always what they should be. People do suffer unjustly. Nevertheless, whenever we have been the contributors to uncomfortable circumstances, we must accept our share of the responsibility. To do otherwise would be dishonest.

We live in a universe that is governed by law. There is a cause-and-effect relationship between you and how the universe treats you.

When people feel unwanted, unloved, and unappreciated, they try to compensate by new relationships with new friends. Often they change jobs and even careers looking for happiness. But old problems are not solved by new surroundings. Most of the problems that we face in life occur because we fail to adjust properly to the environment around us. Simply changing our environment is not the solution. We need to first address the real problem—the re-creation of the self.

You create the circumstances that are around you—

good or bad. You are broadcasting a message to the world that reveals how you want to be treated. No one can violate your well-being unless you have given your prior approval.

The world doesn't put a price on you—you do. You are telling the world what you are worth. Whatever price you set, the world will pay.

It is a tragedy that so many people underestimate their own worth. They neither understand nor realize their dignity and potential.

The circumstances around you are created by your attitude toward yourself, life, others, and God. If you feel that you are inferior, cheap, and unworthy, the world around you will pick up that message and will treat you in just that way. If you feel that life is unfair and that the world owes you a living, then life will treat you unfairly and deny you any living. If you think that people are vicious and cruel, then that is the way they will treat you. If in your mind God is involved in all of this mistreatment, then you are going to turn more and more inward, further complicating an already bad situation.

Be careful of what you are broadcasting, because the world around you will send back to you the feelings and attitudes that you send out.

Illness, loneliness, and many other negative conditions can be reflections of negative thinking.

Every condition of life begins with an idea. Ideas are the roots of all subsequent circumstances. Be careful of the ideas that you entertain, because every idea is a seed that will sooner or later bless or curse you. All the circumstances that surround you began as an idea that you sheltered, nurtured, and brought into reality.

In his letter to the Philippian church, the apostle Paul said, "Fix your thoughts on what is true and good and right. Think about things that are pure and lovely, and dwell on the fine good things in others. Think about all you can praise God for and be glad about." (Philippians 4:8, Living Bible).

The apostle Paul knew that good ideas bring blessing into reality and bad ideas carry misery and suffering.

This is an immutable law—every idea that finds a home in you will become part of your reality. Think about anything long enough and it will be yours—good or bad.

The hypochondriac lives in an atmosphere of illness and thus recurrently creates not just the possibility of an illness but the actual illness itself. The solution for the hypochondriac is wholesale regeneration. The birth of a changed attitude is the key to health. People have said to me over the years, "... but I don't want to be this way." Yet they are looking to the doctors or someone else to change the circumstances that only they can change. The real illness is in the mind and can be addressed only through a change in the thought processes. The bad idea of recurrent illness must be replaced by the positive idea of health and wholeness.

Poverty is another circumstance to which people surrender, and yet the root cause is still an idea. "I am no good," "Nothing good ever happens to me," "I am a born loser," and similar concepts all keep people in the poverty trap. It is even worse when we make God the creator and keeper of the trap. There are many sincere people who believe that poverty is God's way of keeping us spiritual. They believe that the less they have, the more they will depend upon God to meet their needs. Some religious systems require their followers to take vows of poverty, renouncing all earthly possessions, and then they are forced to beg for their daily needs; or at the least, depend upon someone else for their sustenance. This is not spirituality—this is an absurdity. No one becomes more spiritual by placing his or her problems on others. Spirituality is found by solving your own problems.

As long as people think "poor" they will be poor. On the other hand, let them think of the wealth of the universe that their Father has placed at their disposal, and they have taken the first step out of the poverty trap.

Loving acceptance is another circumstance that starts as an idea. If you treat others with love, they will in turn be loving to you. In the Sermon on the Mount (Matt. 7:12) Jesus Christ said, "Therefore all things whatsoever ye would that men should do to you, do ye even so to them." Many times in business, marriages, or social contacts hard feelings have existed between two or more people. Sooner or later, someone goes to the other party apologetically, only to have the other party apologize to them. But if you are aloof, insincere, cold, and indifferent, that is how others will treat you. Most people who mistreat others have never learned to accept themselves. It is not that they are unsure of others; they are unsure of themselves. The world around them senses that insecurity and returns it to them. If you want to be loved, then be loving to others. If you want many friends, then be friendly to others. But all of this starts with an idea, "I am worthwhile and deserve friends, and others are worthwhile and deserve my friendship."

All these examples illustrate the fact that we can

control many of our circumstances; they should not control us.

So when you find yourself in circumstances that are uncomfortable, don't try to change the circumstances. You may succeed in changing them, but the change will be only temporary. Deal with the cause and not with the symptoms. Change those things in your life that created the undesirable circumstances, and then those circumstances will disappear, never to recur.

I have known individuals who repeatedly failed at business ventures because they had no confidence in their own abilities. They were great planners and dreamers, but when they got to the implementation stage, they got cold feet. However, by people's pointing out to them little successes that they had overlooked, they began to develop the confidence that perhaps they could accomplish something big. You can't possibly succeed in anything if you are hounded by a fear of failing or by a lack of belief in yourself.

The philosopher William James often pointed out that simply the belief itself that something is possible brings success. Belief in yourself and your abilities is a positive force that not only creates opportunities for success but makes success itself a reality.

Just as bad circumstances are caused by bad ideas and attitudes, good circumstances are caused by good ideas and attitudes. Therefore, purge from your life all negative and inferior ideas and replace them with positive and superior ideas. The mind, just as the home, needs occasional housecleaning.

The secret of successful Christian living is the dynamism of faith. Positive people accomplish good more easily than negative people. Negativity destroys, and faith creates.

So do as Paul said and fill your life with positive ideas. Then your circumstances will be conducive to growth and happiness.

By God, you can do it.

# CHAPTER 7

# *The Power of an Idea*

Nothing ever begins until someone gets an idea. Nor does anything change without an idea. Ideas are at the root of all growth in life. Without ideas, life itself would not be possible.

One of the greatest sources of power available to any person is the mind. Yet we both take it for granted and overlook its potential.

All of the great discoveries of history, including the most modern scientific achievements, began as simple ideas. Great music, great art, great writing, all started as simple sparks in someone's mind.

Nature itself is the prototype upon which many inventions have been built. Ancient man must have seen the wind blowing objects across the water and developed an idea that ships could be driven by sails catching the wind. Certainly the flight of birds inspired man to study aerodynamics and conceive of machines that could fly. It is a long way from Kitty Hawk, North Carolina, to Americans walking on the moon, but every step in between is the by-product of someone's idea.

Everyone has ideas, but only those who recognize their potential and think boldly bless us with inventions and advance the cause of society. The real power then is not just in having ideas but in learning what kind of ideas to have and how to use them once they come to us.

Ideas like anything else in life can be good or bad. In any circumstance there are always many options possible. Some we think of ourselves. Some are laid at our feet by other "helpful" people. But we must be selective about the ideas that are presented to us and the ideas that we develop on our own. The ideas that we adopt will determine the course of our lives.

When any idea is presented to us, we must determine if that idea will lead to good or bad results. It is after all really the results in which we are interested. Ideas necessarily lead to actions, and actions always end in results. Therefore, we must be careful of the ideas that we entertain.

"I think I am catching a cold" is an idea that most often results in the catching of a cold. First of all, we are recognizing the existence of a condition that we do not ordinarily desire. Secondly, we are saying that this undesirable state is probably going to be ours. Thirdly, we are dooming ourselves to be the hapless victim of an outside force. The running sinuses, the sneezes, the discomfort all become very real—but they all started as an idea, "I think I am catching a cold."

Rejecting the concept of a cold is much better than inviting the cold. Either possibility is within our control, and both are ideas, neither of which is necessarily more powerful than the other. In other words—you can accept or reject the suggestion "I am getting a cold." The end result is dependent upon your actions. We shall return to this topic in a later chapter.

Great people have great ideas. Superior people have superior ideas. Average people have average ideas. Small people have small ideas. These statements seem to suggest that people are great or small and thus have ideas that match what they are. This is not so. It is our ideas that determine who we really are, not the other way around. No one can think big and stay small. You and everything about you will mirror the ideas you have. The only real difference between the genius and the ordinary person is the types of ideas each produces.

One of the greatest contributions to personal success, then, seems to be the ability to think big. Big ideas make big people. We may start out the same, but those who think boldly are those who rise to the top.

Unfortunately, the negativity of others sometimes destroys those who are able to think "big." Negative ideas dropped into young minds will invariably destroy or at least thwart that person's potential. Children with very high I.Q.'s have often been mistaken for being average or retarded simply because some evaluator had a bad day or was professionally incompetent. This is tragic; the truth is, children do not fail—systems do.

It may at first seem overly simplistic to say that big ideas produce big people, but it is abundantly clear that more people have the capacity for entertaining big ideas than there are those who actually have big ideas. It is equally clear that "thinking small" keeps people from realizing their potential. Furthermore, there are enough cases on record to prove that people who change their self-image from negative to positive and then allow their God-given creativity to soar immediately begin to rise above others who are reluctant to do the same.

Two vital qualities are required for personal success through the proper use of ideas.

1. First, we must be positive people who use positive ideas. Anybody can destroy. That is negativity. But only positive people build. Those who live on fear or who invariably expect the worst will never go far in life. They criticize those who succeed and often curse the fates that denied them the benefits others enjoy. They bathe themselves in self-pity. Negative people can never be trusted in a crisis. Because they have no confidence in themselves, they become lost in the conflict. They know nothing good is going to happen to them, and that very attitude literally makes them right. Ideas are like magnets, and they attract to us the things we imagine. A long time ago the biblical character Job said, "That which I feared came upon me." (Job 3:25)

Positive people get results. They attract other people. They have a good rapport with others and instill confidence wherever they go. They offer solutions to problems, while those who are negative see only the problems.

Furthermore, the ideas of positive people will be positive and will elicit other positive ideas from those around them. This kind of positivism is contagious. It spreads through groups and businesses, helping others to release their potentials. A "wet blanket" will be totally out of place in such a group.

2. The second vital quality for personal success is the ability to think big. Big ideas bring big results. Why think small and produce small when the same

amount of thought applied to big ideas can bring big results? The amount of thought that we use does not determine success; rather success depends on the content of our ideas. It is just as easy to make a million dollars as it is to make ten thousand dollars. The difference is not in our efforts but rather in the goals that we adopt and the ideas that we use to reach those goals. We really need to entertain audacious ideas if we are ever to rise above average. God is a big God, and people who really want to be godlike must learn to think big. True spirituality is found in the bigness of our ideas, not in some religious tradition. Yet the bigness of our ideas has never been a criterion used by theologians or religion to measure spirituality. Perhaps that reveals why theologians and religions have so little impact upon the actual advance of society.

If you want to grow, start thinking bigger than you ever have before. Be positive, knowing that God will bless and honor you if you dare to use your God-given abilities to reach your God-given potentials. You may not accomplish all that you desire, but you certainly will accomplish far more than the person with lesser goals. It is not tragic not to reach your goals. It is tragic to have no goals.

People with big ideas accomplish big things.

By God, you can do it.

# CHAPTER 8

# *Law Runs All of Life*

We live in a universe ruled by law. From ancient times mankind has recognized the relationships of causes and effects. We often think these laws apply only to things in nature, such as planets and their orbits, but law applies to all of life. Law is involved in the success of the businessman just as it is involved in the poverty of the financial failure.

It is easy to believe that those who succeed are the beneficiaries of lucky breaks and those who have not succeeded were denied those lucky breaks. The naïve may think that "good fortune" depends on luck, but success in life takes a lot more than luck. The reason that "the rich get richer and the poor get poorer," as the saying goes, is law. Each is following the path of law even if he is not aware of it.

From the start we must rule out the belief that God assigns wealth or the absence thereof to people. God does not discriminate. The person who looks to God to place the blame for disappointments in life looks in vain. In no way does God name people for success or failure, riches or poverty, heaven or hell.

In some ways it may be spiritually fulfilling to think that God assigns us to certain levels of living. But the Scriptures assure us that "God...giveth to all men liberally" (James 1:5). Elsewhere (James 4:2) it says, "Ye have not, because ye ask not." The clear teaching of the Scriptures is that it is God's will for mankind to be more blessed than the average person has been. Two thousand years of misconception and pseudo-spirituality have denied us our heritage as children of God. It is my hope that this book will reorient your thinking toward all the positive things God has for you.

The conditioning for success or the lack thereof usually starts in the childhood years. Unfortunately, negative thinking is extremely difficult to change at a later date. Give any child a sin phobia, teach him or her that Christians can't be popular in this world or that Christians can't expect much in this life, and you will have thwarted much of the God-given potential in that child. The worst influence that any adult can have on any child is to place negativity in the child's mind. This is just another illustration that shows that life is run by law.

The Scriptures give us insight into the 'lawfulness' of all life. "As a twig is bent, so the tree will grow." "Be not deceived; God is not mocked: for whatsoever a man soweth, that shall he also reap" (Gal. 6:7).

We know that on a physical level you reap in a garden whatever you sow. If you want tomatoes, you must plant tomatoes. You do not sow corn and reap tomatoes. Nature, created by God, is too law abiding for that. You get back whatever you put in.

*44*

God has built law into all of life and its circumstances. No one can violate God's law and continue to be blessed. If you want to live a blessed life, then you must learn to follow God's law of blessings. That lesson is just as clear as any other law of nature.

The most basic law about people has already been quoted. "As he thinketh in his heart, so is he" (Prov. 23:7). Whatever kind of thought you have about yourself and life invariably determines what kind of circumstances you will live in. Thoughts are like magnets and will attract to the person the conditions that are first and foremost in his or her mind. If you live in a constant fear of illness, you will be a sick person. On the other hand, if you live a life that is full of optimism and hope, you will be a blessed and happy person. This is an immutable law. Like attracts like. Your thoughts predetermine almost everything in which you are involved.

There is a spiritual law that teaches

THINK ABOUT ANYTHING LONG
ENOUGH, AND YOU WILL CREATE
THE POSSIBILITY OF THAT THING—
GOOD OR BAD.

Job 3:25 says, "The thing which I greatly feared came upon me." Modern medicine has given great blessings, but there are also some inherent dangers as well. Medicine wants us to be aware of illness and the symptoms of illness, BUT IT DOES NOT WANT US TO BE PREOCCUPIED WITH ILLNESS. There are those people who are already psychologically inclined toward illness. For this type of person a little knowledge is a dangerous thing. I have met people who could read the symptoms of a brand-new disease in the morning paper, and they would have the symptoms before the evening papers were out. Preoccupation with illness creates an atmosphere in which illness and disease can flourish. This is part of the law-abiding universe that God has given us. The laws of God were given to us for good, but the abuse or misuse thereof brings grief.

Law governs business success and failure. The person who feels good about himself, who cooperates with the laws of success and works hard for that success, will find success sooner or later. Contrast that with the attitude "Nothing good ever happens to me," and you will see why nothing good can happen to the person with that attitude. He has blocked the pathway to success and instead has invited failure into his life.

PEOPLE WHO REFUSE TO DO
SOMETHING TO CHANGE THEIR
UNDESIRABLE CIRCUMSTANCES WILL
FIND THEMSELVES INSEPARABLY
CHAINED TO THOSE
CIRCUMSTANCES.

Successful people get ahead in life because they believe in themselves and have discovered the immutable law that empowers them to take control of their lives. Too many people are waiting for that lucky break or for someone to do something for them. Successful people know that if you want anything in life, you have to work to get it and to keep it. Even those who are born to affluence learn sooner or later that they must work to maintain it or it will be gone.

Successful people succeed because they have about

them the aura of success. They think it. They feel it. They live it and breathe it. Such people may have occasional setbacks, but the statement "You can't keep a good person down," refers to them.

On the other hand, people who fail in life must seek out the causes of their failure. When we are honest about ourselves, where we are and what we are, then we are beginning to leave the path of disappointment and open the doorway to change. To sit in self-pity and gloom only further complicates an already hopeless circumstance.

There are laws that govern every successful venture in life, and they will guarantee success. The wise person learns them as soon as possible and utilizes them to the maximum. The concept that Darwin applied to nature, namely that only the fit survive, was a law that he had previously observed in everyday life. Every successful person can testify to the efficacy of that law. Managers, administrators, business people, and many others know that disaster is invited when such laws are violated.

Law determines everything. We live in a law-abiding universe, created by a law-giving God, and to live successfully is to fully cooperate with and utilize those laws. There are no shortcuts. As in civil life, the criminal mind sooner or later will be caught and punished.

Let me spell out some of the laws upon which life is built, that God has given to us.

1. The way you feel about yourself determines what you receive in life.

2. The way you feel about life, determines how life treats you.

3. The way that you feel about others determines how others treat you.

4. Successful people believe in themselves and in the results of investing themselves in something worthwhile.

5. A preoccupation with sickness produces a sick mind and a sick body.

6. A healthy mind radiates wholeness to the entire being and prevents illness.

7. In any undesirable circumstance, people with positive attitudes come out better than those with negative attitudes.

8. The attitudes that we broadcast to life are invariably reflected back to us.

9. God is on the side of law and order. Follow His laws and you will succeed.

These are not all the laws that govern life. Every person can add to the list from his or her own discoveries, but they give us a good start.

Realize that you, and all the world, are bound by immutable law. Work with those laws that will bring happiness and peace to you and avoid those negative ideas that spell disaster. When you work with the laws of God, you are working with God Himself. Put those laws above religion and other man-made misconceptions, and you will discover true spirituality. Work with God, and God will work with you.

That's what I mean when I say,

"By God, you can do it."

CHAPTER 9

# *Imaging*

$A$n old Chinese proverb claimed that one picture is worth a thousand words. A mental picture is worth even more. It often spells the difference between success and failure, illness or health, happiness or sadness.

Imaging is not imagination. Don't confuse the two because there is a profound difference. Imagination can conjure up anything. I can imagine myself as the king of France or a famous movie star. But such thoughts, in defiance of reality, are a waste of time, since they fail to produce results.

Imaging, on the other hand, is simply holding a mental picture. We all store mental pictures in our minds. The yard at Grandma's, the creek where we used to walk, the street in front of our house, the face of an old friend, and many more wonderful scenes delight us as we watch them on the mental television of the inner eye. No one can be faulted for finding respite from the cares of the adult world by flashbacks to earlier and more pleasant days. These mental pictures, indelibly inscribed in our minds, give us roots and security.

Imaging also clarifies our goals. Artists, architects, draftsmen, and others who draw up plans for projects all use mental pictures. I know of an architect who designs houses for isolated places. He will go to the site and sit for hours building mental pictures until he finds the combination that just fits the scene. Then he will go home and sketch the house for the owner's approval. If something isn't quite right he says, "But that's not quite the way I saw it," and he will make changes until he gets it right.

Still, there is a dark side to mental pictures that we must recognize. Due to our psychological makeup, traumas are etched more deeply than pleasant times. The scene of an accident, the face of a criminal, and many other psychological scars burn pictures that can never be erased. We may experience them as flashbacks as we fall asleep, or they may be triggered by similar events or circumstances. Sometimes even intensive therapy under professional supervision cannot erase these scars. Other times people can handle the problem but they say, "Try as I might I cannot erase that picture from my mind. I see it when I close my eyes. . . . I am afraid to fall asleep because I keep seeing it over and over."

One indicator of mental health is the selection of mental pictures we choose to hold in front of us. The troubled adult may live in the past, playing in Grandma's yard where a feeling of safety prevailed, or avoid the pain of recurring traumatic memories by retreating into a shell in a state of dysfunction.

CONSTRUCTIVE IMAGING IS
HOLDING A MENTAL PICTURE OF
SOMETHING THAT WE WISH TO
ACCOMPLISH. IT IS ESTABLISHING A
GOAL AND KEEPING THAT PICTURE
BEFORE OUR MINDS UNTIL IT IS
FULFILLED, MODIFIED OR
SURRENDERED.

Such mental pictures do accomplish several things.

1. Rather than drift through a segment of life, we have a goal that we wish to reach.

2. All of our mental forces concentrate upon bringing that goal into reality, thus focusing our efforts.

3. We avoid the lure of distractions by being preoccupied with our goal.

4. The preoccupation with our goal insulates us from the negative influence of doubts and the discouraging comments of others who choose to drift through life taking whatever comes along.

Let's examine several instances of the proper usage of imaging.

1. Suppose that we have suffered an injury, such as a sprain or a broken arm or leg, and the period of healing has ended, the cast is removed, and we are told we can now try that part of our body again; or perhaps a stroke has occurred that left us with a disability, and we are in therapy.

The proper usage of imaging will produce a picture of that portion of our body, an arm, a leg, or an internal organ as functioning properly. We will see that crippled hand working perfectly or that ankle or leg as being strong and normal. Every time we have therapy or are practicing complete recovery, we keep that image before us. It is the magnet that draws to us the desired goal.

The model is the perfect plan of God—the way a normal arm, leg, or organ usually functions. We keep telling ourselves that God is the creator of our bodies, that He has designed them and His love is given to us and His power is at work in us. We will accept nothing less than His perfect plan being accomplished within us.

If we keep before us the image of that part of our body as functioning properly, then work in therapy to completely accomplish and actualize that picture, we will achieve our goal despite the labor and the pain. Once again, it is the attitude that makes possible the healing. That is true faith healing.

Contrast this attitude with that of the person who has been told to accept and live with some negative condition. Once you have accepted an image of incapacity you will never regain the normal function of the original divine design.

A woman once asked me to pray for her arthritis. I probably shocked her when I said, "Your arthritis seems to be doing quite well without my prayers. I will pray instead for your wholeness."

I have known of dozens of cases where people overcame physical problems through the power of prayer, imaging, and therapy. Cancers have been cured, damaged hearts have been reconstructed, arthritic limbs have been renewed, literally the lame have been made to walk—all through the combination of imaging, prayer, therapy, and faith. We shall explore this topic more fully in a later chapter.

2. Another example of imaging is illustrated by the

accomplishment of a physical goal, such as an athletic event. Some years ago a world class high jumper, an Olympic star, explained his success by saying that he stayed at the end of the runway where his approach to the bar was to begin until he could envision his body soaring over the untouched bar. Then he would begin his run. Contrast that vision of success with the attitude of defeat. "I can't do it" has defeated the effort before it was even made.

Much success in life is built on the mental precondition "By God, I can do it." The person with that kind of faith can literally move mountains.

Athletes in all areas of sports have testified that they found success in their endeavors only after they started holding mental pictures of the desired success. Their testimonies are clear-cut because it is easy to see success or failure on the athletic field, while it is not always as easy to see it in life. Nevertheless, the image of success invariably makes people successful, while the image of defeat invariably spells doom.

3. Another example of imaging is the successful acquisition of a career goal. Perhaps we wish to attain a certain career or a certain level in our chosen career. Perhaps we wish to have a certain income by a set age or acquire a certain level of savings by the time that we retire.

The mere adoption of such an image is never enough. We must work toward the realization of those images. If I wish to be the treasurer of a big corporation but I refuse to study and reach the level of qualification necessary for that appointment, I am not being realistic. If I spend all my money in unwise ways, I will never accumulate any savings.

But notice what it means to have no image before

me. It means that I have no goals and maybe no ambitions. Without these, I won't go anywhere.

The easy availability of modern education has encouraged many women to begin their college work after they have raised their families. Some have been grandmothers before they went to college. Retirees and others have gone back to college to learn a new career. All these people have the image of a goal before them whether it is a college degree or the successful transfer to a new career. The image of the desired goal inspires them. It gives them courage when uninspired people simply give up. No wonder the Bible says, "Where there is no vision, the people perish" (Prov. 29:18).

No one ever stumbles into success. It is found only in the fulfillment of a certain image, a certain goal. People who learn to image their way through each stage of their development soon come to understand the divine laws of creation. They know the power of an idea. They can learn to control their circumstances. Most of all, they learn to work with God.

No wonder Jesus Christ said, "What things soever ye desire, when ye pray, believe that ye receive them, and ye shall have them" (Mark 11:24).

Imaging is a tool for success. It is not the only tool, but like any other tool, it makes accomplishing the job a lot easier. Long-term goals or short-term goals are all open to the wholesome influence of faith when imaging is properly applied. This is God's law of creation.

There is tremendous power in an idea. Imaging is the focusing of your ideas to accomplish a desired goal.

Whatever goal you have in life, create for yourself an image of that goal being accomplished. Forget your own doubts and fears. Don't listen to the negativity of those who would dissuade or discourage you. Realize that in this quest, God is your partner. You are not alone. Keep working, praying, believing for the full accomplishment of your goal and let nothing turn you aside.

Perhaps you may not reach that exact goal. Perhaps, along the way, you may change your mind about the desired goal. But you will still be a better person for having tried and failed than the person who never tried at all. In the long run you will have won even if you do not completely fulfill your goal.

Whatever goal you do reach, you will reach it more rapidly and with less effort if you hold the image of that accomplished goal before you.

Learn to image. Imaging makes things easier. It is part of God's plan of success.

By God, you can do it.

CHAPTER 10

# *Make Good Things Happen in Your Life*

*B*y now you should be putting together some of the preceding concepts to form new ideas of what life can be like if you use all the powers that God has given to you. Imaging, for example, in co-operation with God's laws, will create new ideas about your circumstances and yourself. In this chapter we are going to explore the concept of making good things happen. Since we have that ability, we might as well use it.

Very little good comes to the person who simply takes what life hands out. Life is designed so that the person who takes charge of life, cooperating with all the laws of God, will go farther and be healthier and happier than the person who sits back and takes whatever comes along.

No one ever said that life is fair. It is a war out there. The land of indecision, no-man's-land, is not the place to be. We have to be aggressive if we desire to survive, and this is a necessary part of spiritual discipline.

It was a popular Christian philosophy at one time to believe that spirituality came through acquiescence, self-denigration, and placidity. That concept was exemplified in such hymns as "Gentle Jesus, Meek and Mild." An overemphasis and misinterpretation was placed on the beatitudes given by Jesus Christ in Matthew 5. The meek were to inherit the earth, so Christians were instructed to be meek. A necessary part of that meekness seemed to be a disinterest in ever rising above one's peers. Rather than stimulate excellence, the trend was toward being average.

There is a great misunderstanding of Christ's use of the word "meek," caused in part by the change that language undergoes over centuries. What Christ was really commending was humility as contrasted with pride and the use of reason rather than force. In other words, the meek person who was to inherit the earth was the quiet and humble person who unobtrusively knew how to get the job done and did it in love.

Hopefully, previous chapters have shown a different concept of spirituality and the will of God for each individual.

I have always been inspired by these words of Longfellow from "The Psalm of Life: What the Heart of the Young Man said to the Psalmist:"

> In the world's broad field of battle,
> In the bivouac of Life,
> Be not like dumb, driven cattle!
> Be a hero in the strife!
> . . . .

Lives of great men all remind us
We can make our lives sublime,
And, departing, leave behind us
Footprints on the sands of time.

That type of dedication is far more spiritual than the attitude of taking whatever life gives us. Spirituality is not a negative concept. It should be measured in terms of action rather than inaction and submission.

1. Before you can make good things happen, you have to have a goal or goals. The absence of a goal puts you back into the old routine of taking whatever comes along. The absence of goals says to the world that either you do not care what happens to you or you are powerless to resist whatever the world chooses to give you.

Goals are just as important for the person who is ninety as the person who is nine, nineteen, or twenty-nine. It is sometimes thought that the planning period of life precedes retirement and that after retirement we simply have no goals other than that of survival. Goals are a necessary force in all phases of life. They are the raison d'être, the "reason to be" for life itself. The lack of goals explains why so many people die immediately following their retirements. Having nothing further to live for, in their opinions, they do the logical thing and die.

Goals organize our energies, direct us toward a certain accomplishment, and help us to plan every step along the way. Many goals are necessary in the successful life. We have long-range goals as well as short-range goals, and successful planning prevents them from conflicting with each other. Part of good mental discipline is the ordering of our goals in clearly defined priorities.

Let's clarify the concept of a goal. By "goal" I simply mean anything that you would like to accomplish. The concept of "a big goal" or "a little goal" is strictly relative. What is a big goal to one person may be a little goal to another. One person may borrow a million dollars to accomplish a goal. To many people, that amount of money would involve a big goal, since they borrow only enough money to buy a new car. There are others, however, who trade in business deals of even larger amounts than a million. To them the million might involve only a small goal.

It is also true that most big goals involve a series of smaller goals. If the big goal for us is to get out of debt, then the series of small goals to accomplish that would be to pay off our store bills, the car loan, the money we borrowed from our parents, etc.

Your goals must always put a challenge before you. Easy goals are not very productive. They do not accomplish much in life. If your goals are smaller than they should be, then you need to raise your level of expectation.

Each person can adopt big goals—and God expects us to do just that. God is not honored through small thinking. In fact, in a way, small thinkers are really blaspheming, because they are denying the power of God to accomplish great things.

God is a God of bigness, and people who think big give more honor to God than the people who think small.

Hebrews 11:6 says, "Without faith, it is impossible to please Him: for he that cometh to God must believe that He is, and that He is a rewarder of them that diligently seek Him."

There is no difference in the amount of power that is used to set small goals or big goals. Since the power that changes the world is truly the power of God, big goals are as easily accomplished as little goals. Therefore, it makes sense to set big goals for ourselves, because they will accomplish more than small goals.

No wonder the Bible puts so much emphasis upon dreamers. Those who can dream will accomplish more than those who do not.

Set goals for yourself in every stage of life and dare to make them big.

2. Another important concept is that of being expectant in life. Contrast the attitude that says, "Nothing (good) ever happens to me" with the attitude "I wonder what new thing God is going to show me today."

Expectancy opens the door to blessings, because once we have created the opportunity for blessings they will follow. Expectancy creates the necessary condition in which things can happen.

To begin the day with pessimism or despair is to ruin that day before it starts. The negative person attracts negative and undesirable circumstances. The optimistic, positive, expectant person creates circumstances that are favorable to good things, and thus they occur. Like attracts like. Be positive and draw to your life the good things, for when you are negative you are attracting disaster.

3. Work and discipline are necessary parts of spiritual growth. Some years ago in reading the autobiography of a very successful businessman, I came across these words:

"People were always telling me how lucky I was and how I got all the breaks, but I long since noted that the harder I worked, the luckier I got."

This clearly illustrates spiritual law. God does help those who help themselves. If you want good things to happen to you, work hard for them, and they will. On the other hand, to passively wait for someone else (including God) to solve your problems only prolongs them. None of our problems are ever solved while we wait for someone else (including God) to undertake responsibility for them.

Many sincere but sincerely mistaken people believe their lack of spiritual growth is the fault of someone else. They change churches looking for the right pastor to do for them what they refuse to do for themselves. They are similar to the hypochondriac who blames his continued illness on the ineptness of physicians. I have even seen people blame their lack of spiritual progress on their spouse. "I can't be spiritual living with that person." It is hard work to face ourselves, and take responsibility for the solutions of our own problems, but it is the necessary beginning to the path of spiritual blessings.

If you want good things to happen in your life, then work for them. Study, learn, grow, and you will be amazed at the opportunities that will come your way.

4. The next important concept is that of living each day in a creative partnership with God. It must be both creative and a partnership if it is to succeed.

There is no need for an apology when we live as a positive, creative witness for God. In Romans 1:16 Paul exclaims, "I am not ashamed of the gospel." Paul did not say he was proud of religion, nor did he boast of a church or a denomination. There is a tremendous difference between being religious and being a positive creative witness.

If we live in daily communion with God, constantly aware of His presence, we will be endowed with both a peace and an energy that defies description. This opens the door to a creative partnership where the mind of God literally becomes ours. "Let this mind be in you, which was also in Christ Jesus" (Philippians 2:5).

A relationship with God bores no one, rather it invigorates and inspires. The early Christian martyrs died of many things, but they never died of boredom. Their contagious witness changed the history of civilization and has made possible all the advances known in our modern world. The same benefit continues today.

The person who has goals and is expectant about them, working toward fulfillment in a partnership with God, will invariably make good things happen in life. An expectant life has no room for apathy or resignation. When you are busy in this way, you are drawing good things to yourself blocking out the undesirable. Be aggressive in this program. Makes good things happen to you in life. God has given you this power, and by God, you can do it.

To make good things happen to you,

1. Always have before you a goal or goals toward which you are striving.

2. Be expectant about life and positive about good things happening to you.

3. Work hard to bring your goals and expectations into reality.

4. Remember that you are not alone. God has invited you to be his partner in life.

By God, you can do it.

# CHAPTER 11

# The Foolishness of Carrying Guilt

*I*n chapter two we talked briefly of guilt. We will explore the topic more fully here.

Guilt is the occupational hazard of living in the twentieth century. It seems to grip ninety percent of our population. Regardless of what circumstances John Q. Public finds himself in, he carries guilt about it. If he is affluent, he feels guilty when he sees the poor. If he is poor, he carries guilt over his failure. Everything seems to instill guilt—success or failure, riches or poverty, fame or anonymity.

Unfortunately, we fail to distinguish between judicial guilt and the feeling of guilt. If I fail to stop at a stop sign and the officer gives me a traffic ticket, I can go to court and plead guilty to the charge. That is judicial guilt—I broke a law or some rule imposed by a group. But suppose my failure to stop at the stop sign resulted in an accident, and a child was seriously injured. Now the feeling of guilt over injuring someone is an added burden.

There is another distinction that we must make concerning guilt. Imagined guilt is different from real guilt. If I have injured someone by accident, then I can carry real guilt if it were due to my carelessness. But suppose it was not, or suppose I mistakenly think something was my fault, then the guilt I feel is imagined.

Several years ago I counseled a man who was sixty-five years of age. For the last forty years he had been haunted by a decision that he had made in his mid-twenties. At that time he felt that God wanted him to become a minister, but he refused to do so. For forty years he had carried this weight of guilt, believing that he would be punished in hell for refusing to obey God. He felt doomed both in this life and eternity.

That is a burden of guilt that no one need carry. That guilt kept him from living a full life and living in harmony with God in his maturing years. Such guilt was imagined, not put there by God.

All guilt is self-imposed. It is an attitude that we adopt in the face of certain circumstances. Much guilt is of the judicial type. We believe that we have violated the law of God, just as punishable as man's law. Because of this violation we believe that we stand irrevocably condemned before the bar of divine justice. In a preceding chapter we have discussed the concept of sin. The biblical concept of sin is God's way of offering us his help. To be a sinner in the biblical sense merely means that we are never going to make it on our own and that God wants to help us.

Many sincere people think that they must confess sin after sin, groveling in a spiritually counterproductive self-denigration in order to earn salvation. I have known people who invented "sins" in order to have something to confess. The attitude seemed to be that the greater their sense of sin, the more the Lord would be impressed with their need and their sincerity.

Such a preoccupation with guilt and sin is counterproductive and prevents a person from maturing spiritually.

If you think you can pay for your sins, buy or earn your salvation, or believe that you can make yourself good enough for God, then you fully misunderstand the biblical message of the Love of God.

The cure for judicial guilt is simply to accept the biblical concept of forgiveness extended to you by God freely and unequivocally. You may still feel unworthy—but who is worthy? God is giving His love to all, and He set the conditions, not you.

But it is not so easy to deal with guilt that arises from our interactions with others. There are several spiritual guidelines to follow.

1. If you can correct something wrong that you did, then it will be to your spiritual benefit to correct it. If you told a lie about someone or if you said something bad about someone and it is in your power to correct it, then take action.

2. Some things in the past should just be forgotten. This is particularly true if the injured party is not around for you to correct the misdeed. But remember that no one has a license to hurt someone else. Sometimes bringing up the past does more harm than good. There comes a time when we have to learn to let go. It is foolish to try to relive the past in order to correct it. No one ever advances spiritually by trying to re-enter the past. The past is gone and should be accepted as such. We learn from it, but we do not try to relive it.

66

All sins, including the sin of hurting another, are covered in the forgiveness of God. If we have hurt someone and it is impossible to correct the situation, then the best thing to do is to simply forget it. Nothing will be gained by being preoccupied with our misdeeds. The message of the Bible is the message of forgiveness, not of guilt and condemnation. Once we have asked for God's forgiveness, it is freely given. Thus we can let go of the guilt that often burdens us. Don't deny yourself the joy of God's victory for today by reliving the defeats of yesterday.

3. If we have done something contrary to the will of God, then the will of God is constantly changing to bring it in line with the present circumstances. This is why imagined guilt is so unnecessary. If it was the will of God for the aforementioned man to become a minister, and he refused to do so, it doesn't mean that God dropped him from all further relationships. God would then bring another plan into reality, because there are always alternatives. I know little of what the man did for those forty years other than live in absolute misery. But let's suppose that he had become a mechanic or a carpenter. Then God's will would have been that he be the best he could be at his chosen career.

We seem to have a mistaken notion that the best witness for God is made from the pulpit and only clergy people serve God. Nothing could be further from the truth. The best witness for God is made by those people who in everyday life witness to His power by their lives and actions in the real world.

The man previously mentioned had tricked himself into an inability to witness because he thought he had violated God's will for his life. His greater tragedy was the inability to forget the past and to adjust to the thrill of living each day with a new hope.

4. There is an additional imagined guilt that we cannot fully isolate. It haunts people who believe that they have done something horrible but they don't know what it is. I have counseled with those who have told me that they had committed the unpardonable sin, but none of them was able to tell me what it was. Nonetheless, the great weight of their guilt was very real.

This type of guilt is really a symptom of another problem. Usually this person is insecure, has been denied a truly loving realtionship, has a tremendous inferiority complex compounded by a bad self-image. In other words, he has never accepted himself and thus feels he has not been accepted by God.

Without trying to be too complex, the only person that God cannot help is the person who refuses to let God help him. That is the unpardonable sin. All other sins can be and are pardoned.

The fact that a person feels unworthy of God's acceptance has nothing to do with God, as God's acceptance is a gift.

God does not confer His love only upon those who have performed spectacular deeds. His blessings are for all, regardless of their so-called standing in life.

Like the pre-Reformation Martin Luther in his monastic cell, you may flagellate your back with a whip to pay for your sins, but don't expect God to wield the whip. He has totally forgiven and accepted you. Learn to accept yourself as a child of God and rejoice in your new standing, demonstrating to others a life truly changed by the love of God. Be the new person that you can be in Christ.

5. God does not hold you responsible for others' situations in life. Despite the fact that we would like to help others, not everybody is ready to be helped. When you try to force spiritual growth on a person who is not ready for it, you will probably do more harm than good. In any given society, there will be those who choose to fail or, at least, who choose not to rise as high as they could. It is not your responsibility to invade their privacy and impose your standards on them. Part of the concept of love includes the ability to allow others to be themselves and to accept them as they are. Instead of carrying guilt because others are not as you would have them to be, love them as they are. Sooner or later, that love will be productive.

Guilt is counterproductive to spiritual growth. Don't try to live in it. Accept these guidelines, given again in summary:

1. Correct any wrong that you have committed as long as it does not cause greater harm to correct it.

2. Realize that all wrong is forgiven in and through the love of God.

3. What cannot be corrected should be confessed in prayer and then forgotten.

4. Don't deny yourself the pleasure of living with God in the present by being preoccupied about the past.

5. Don't feel guilty about where you are in life in comparison to others. Live your own life ministering to others in any way you can.

Get rid of guilt. It is a weight you need not carry. By God, you can do it.

# CHAPTER 12

# *Learning to Accept Yourself*

*A*lmost everybody wishes they were somebody else. Nobody seems to be happy being who they are. Conduct a "man-on-the-street" interview giving people the choice of being anybody in the past or present, and almost nobody would reply that he chooses to be himself. The proverbial grass is always greener on the other side of the fence. Somebody else's life is always happier, more exciting, more desirable.

This suggests two things about modern society.

1. Most people find themselves bored beyond belief. Various statistics have estimated that 80 percent of Americans are bored by their chosen careers. The average person feels put upon and out of control of his or her life. This boredom translates into unhappiness, which reveals why we spend so much money on entertainment in a quest for happiness.

2. Many people dislike themselves. Years ago a young lady came to me in what should have been the prime

of life and said to me, "I hate myself, I hate my body— I hate everything about me." Though this is an extreme example, it is a tragedy that reveals the inner turmoil facing many people.

For a few moments, forget everything that is negative or undesirable about your life and ask yourself, "Why am I the person that I am?"

You are a unique individual. No one else in the entire world is just like you. Several facts prove this.

From a biological point of view, no one else in the entire world has the combination of genes and chromosomes you have, in the way that you have them. From your parents, and they from their parents before them, ad infinitum, you have received a unique combination of those biological factors that determine such things as size, shape, skeletal structure, blood type, intelligence levels, and so forth. Just as no one else in the entire world has the same set of fingerprints that you have, no one else has your physical, emotional, and intellectual characteristics. Geneticists tell us that the possible variations of genes and chromosomes form combinations so great that they approach infinity. You are truly unique.

Add to the biological factors sociological concepts, and the impossibility of duplication increases. Influences such as the home in which you were raised, the family that you had around you, the friends that you played with, the people who touched your life, the various loves to which you have been exposed, and many more considerations, and your uniqueness is even further dramatized. Then add geographical elements such as the country in which you were raised (mountains, valley, rural, urban, etc.) and other experiences you have enjoyed or endured in life, and the impossibility of finding another "you" becomes even more apparent.

Now reflect on the following statement:

I am not an accident.

You are the creation of a loving God. How you got here and the influences that have touched your life may define your past but need not dictate your future. I have talked with people, both men and women, who carry deep scars because of some question about their birth. Some were born of single mothers, some were born resulting from a rape, and others were born into still other stressful situations. One young man traced his difficult life to the fact that his parents wanted no more children, but one night "they slipped." After his birth he was looked upon as "our mistake." Others felt unwanted because their parents gave them up for adoption or were declared unfit.

Few people who have not been through it themselves can truly sympathize with a person who has suffered a trauma through early childhood and subsequent development. There is an unconscious hurt that may never be healed. Professional help and great spiritual experiences are often not enough to overcome these problems.

If any of this is part of your problem, read these words carefully:

YOU ARE NOT AN ACCIDENT, AND IT
IS UNIMPORTANT HOW YOU GOT
HERE. ONCE YOU ARE HERE, YOU
ARE ON THE SAME LEVEL WITH
EVERYBODY ELSE, AS GOOD AS

ANYBODY ELSE, AND YOUR FUTURE
LIES SOLELY WITHIN YOUR
CONTROL.

Once the biological fact of conception was completed, the laws of life then took over to bring you into this world on the same basis as anybody else. God is not in favor of rape, but the child that may issue from that act is as much loved and cared for by God as any other child. People do make mistakes. Doctors are human, and they, too, make mistakes, sometimes resulting in birth injuries, but none of this lessens the worth of any baby born into this world. It is true that all babies are created equal.

Why are you the way you are? Because God wanted a person just like you in the world to show the world that any obstacle can be overcome. The world needed you to perfect itself.

Given all things that make you the person you are, there is something you can give to the world no one else can possibly duplicate. There are things you can do, love you can share, lives you can influence for God that no one else can touch in exactly the same way.

Only one of us is going to be a Michelangelo or a Verdi, but that doesn't mean that there is no place for you. It also doesn't mean that they are more important than you. You are needed as you are, or you wouldn't be here.

Stop longing to be someone else. Stop trying to be someone else. If God had wanted you to be someone else, then He would have created you as someone else. God created you as the person you are because that is the person God and the world needed.

I repeat—how you get here is unimportant. All that

really matters is that you are here. Now what are you going to do about it? Let me make several suggestions.

1. Accept yourself as you are right now. Realize your own worth, your own value, and appreciate your uniqueness. Remember that you can never get anywhere if you don't know where you are now. Accept yourself as you are and where you are. God has already accepted you, so start your growth by accepting the person He has created you to be.

2. Realize the uniqueness of your talents and abilities in combination with your physical living conditions. There are things you can do that no one else can do. There are lives that you can touch that no one else can touch. All of this is part of God's creative potential for you.

YOU ARE TRULY A UNIQUE PERSON—
LIVE IT.

3. Every person has deep within himself or herself an unfathomed ocean of potentiality. There are many things that you can do that you have not yet done. Education is by far the greatest discovery of ability. Make up your own mind that you will not rest until you have explored all the treasures that God has placed within you. You don't have to enroll in formal classes to benefit from education. Maybe you can study at home or in informal groups, but you can always learn more than you now know.

Sometimes one's potential is discovered only after another career has been accomplished. Many women discover new careers after raising a family. Hobbies can sometimes become productive businesses. Relaxing pastimes may be the source of additional income.

Businessmen often retire only to find a new career that brings more fulfillment than their previous career.

Thus there are many reasons for accepting yourself as you now are. Trying to be somebody else can only bring bitter dissapointment and increased frustration. Start where you are—as you are. Accept your present self as the starting point and then let the power of God help you to soar to lofty heights. God can do great things through you, but he can't do anything unless you are willing to let him.

In the next chapter we will find ways to discover the real you, but you must start by accepting yourself as you are.

If you have never prayed this prayer of thanksgiving before, pray it now.

"Father, I thank you that I am the person that you have created. I now accept myself, and I thank you for me."

By God, you can do it.

CHAPTER 13

# The "You"
# Inside You

*Y*ou are unique. There is no one in the world just like you. Use your individuality as God has intended for you to use it. Make yourself happy, and you will make the world around you a better place for others.

Life will be what you make it. All of us must learn this lesson. The potential within you must be released if it is to be realized.

Too many people are reluctant to turn themselves loose. Their hesitation is probably due to one of the following:

1. They don't feel that what they have to offer is very good, or

2. They don't feel important enough to be noticed, or

3. They don't feel the results will be worth the effort.

The great American game is "putting yourself

down." We have been brainwashed into a perverted form of false humility. The average person tries to be very average, if not lower than average, because he or she feels awkward standing out from the crowd. We desire a corporate security where the homogeneity of the group protects our identity. The only exception we allow ourselves is the hero worship we attach to certain people who excel in sports, entertainment, or life. We satiate our desire to be something through a vicarious relationship with their successes.

But we should learn the meaning of the word humility. It is much misunderstood. It is not denigrating yourself. It is not thinking lowly of yourself.

Simply stated,

> HUMILITY IS THE ABILITY TO
> FORGET YOURSELF.

If a person is egotistical or full of pride, he is not humble. But neither is the neurotic who constantly worries about being inferior.

To be totally preoccupied with yourself, thinking only of your success or failure, is a counterproductive activity. The mind can only do so much at a time, and to use your thought processes only for ego-serving purposes is self-destructive.

> HUMILITY IS THE ABILITY TO DO A
> JOB BY TOTALLY DEVOTING
> YOURSELF TO THAT ACTIVITY,
> WITHOUT BEING PREOCCUPIED
> WITH IMAGE, EGO, OR OTHER SELF-
> SERVING THOUGHT PATTERNS.

Another mistake that we often make is comparing ourselves to others. But notice how we do this. We pick out the best in any situation and compare ourselves to that. We compare ourselves to the brightest, the most gifted, or the most successful person in the group, and then when we fall short in the comparison, we immediately conclude that what we have to offer is not comparable and thus we are worthless.

Why don't we compare ourselves to the least successful person in the group or at least to the midpoint or the norm. We would, but that doesn't support the game that we are playing in life. We are already committed to proving our lack of worth, so humility (in the wrong sense) forces us to compare ourselves with the best.

It is foolish to waste time comparing yourself to anybody. Because you are unique, comparison is really impossible. You are not the other person and they are not you, therefore, comparison is pointless. You do not know the inner turmoil of the person you admire. He may have more traumas than you. Secretly he may wish he were you at the same time you are wishing to be him.

Given the range of human abilities, there will always be people who are better in some things than others, but select a different activity and their abilities will shift. There are things that you can do that no one else can do in quite the same way.

Any preoccupation with a comparison between yourself and others only wastes time and thwarts the realization of your own potential.

If these kinds of comparisons have consumed you in the past, abandon the activity now. Practice humility in the good sense of the term and learn to do the job without wasting your time and talents on self-serving worry.

There is a you inside that is worth discovering. If there weren't, you wouldn't be here. The question now is how to discover the real you.

The first step is to examine your own desires, because they are accurate indicators of your inner abilities. What would you like to do? What have you yearned to be for years? What interests you? You have these desires because you have talents and abilities in that direction. Maybe your talents are rough and need to be refined through training or education, but that is to be expected. It is a tragedy that so many people are doing things that don't really interest them when there are other things that they would enjoy doing and would be good at. Take stock of your desires. What is it that really interests you?

Secondly, ask yourself if it is still possible to fulfill these desires. Most people will find that it is, even if the goal requires sacrifices. You may have to give up a secure job to go back to school or to train for another career, but if you can fulfill your dreams, then the cost will be repaid many times over. Perhaps you can train for the new career on a slower schedule while keeping your present employment, or perhaps you can turn a present hobby into a future career.

The third step is to put yourself on a schedule to accomplish your goal. You may have the greatest desires and the ability to fulfill them, but if you never begin, everything else is wasted.

> For all sad words of tongue or pen,
> The saddest are these: "It might have been!"

The most difficult job in any course of action is taking the first step. Once we take that first step, then the spirit of God takes over to encourage and guide us. But he does wait for us to start. Initiating action shows that our desires are not just words but future realities.

One way to discover your talents is to study the needs of the area around you. There will be concerns or convictions that are apparent to you that others will overlook. These concerns will come to you because you have the ability to do something about them. Listen to your concerns. Study your convictions. Then ask yourself if this can be turned into a rewarding involvement on your part—both personally and financially.

Another way of finding your talent is to visit a career counseling center. Modern educational techniques have provided us with a considerable array of tests and other evaluation devices that help people discover their latent talents. The reason that you are the way you are is that God has instilled you with a unique combination of talents and abilities. In part, your happiness will be qualified by the degree to which you fulfill these God-given gifts. Career centers can help determine your abilities and usually can direct you to areas in which your abilities can be fulfilled.

I must give a serious warning, however, to those who tend to jump from one career to another because of a dissatisfaction with their present employment. This dissatisfaction may result from an inability to adjust to stress rather than to the job itself. There may be other emotional causes of our problems, and we mistakenly blame the job. The employment situation mirrors life. If we have not coped adequately with life, we will not cope any better with the job. It would be a serious error to leave a well-paying job because of a personal problem only to find that our problems follow us from job to job.

In short, maybe you, not the job, are the problem. If so, changing jobs solves nothing. You need to change yourself.

No problem is ever solved by running from it. Maturity dictates that we address our problems. Common sense demands that we solve them. Wholeness and health are found in the solution. The inability to solve our problems is part of the illness itself. If you want to treat your illness, then face your problems with the confidence that they will be solved along with the willingness to work at the solution.

Wanting to be whole is part of the solution.

The you inside that you are attempting to discover is basically a loving person. Love is the most powerful force in the world. People love by nature and instinct, but fear or hatred are acquired responses.

I shall devote a later chapter to the concept of love, but you can never discover the real you until you release your capacity to be a warm, loving individual.

God has created life so that those who treat others with love and respect are better people than those who do not. If you want to be the best person you can be, the real you, determine that you will treat everybody you meet with love. The ability to love others will have a profound impact on both you and those you meet.

You will find that love releases your own potential and helps you to be the person that you can be. But love is also reciprocated—and your love will encourage others to be more loving in their own lives. Thus their love will draw from you more of your own potential as you invest yourself in life.

There is a real you inside of you. Each day more of that you will be released as you live with God.

Ponder this thought:

God is unlimited potential—and I can be part of that.

By God, you can do it.

CHAPTER 14

# Self-Forgiveness
# and Self-Love

**G**od thinks more of you than you think of yourself. If you are the average person, you spend the second half of your life correcting the mistakes that you think you made in the first half.

Shakespeare said,

To err is human, to forgive divine.

A more modern philosophy says,

To err is human, to forgive isn't.

Self-forgiveness is the most difficult task anyone ever faces.

I hope that by now you are overcoming some of the self-denigration that commonly plagues our society. You will never realize the potential within you until and unless you realize your own worth.

Jesus Christ said that we are "to love our neighbors

as we love ourselves." Since the average person is not on very good terms with himself or herself, it explains why we don't get along too well with others.

Let me introduce to you a radical concept, one that can truly change your life if you incorporate it into your thinking.

IF YOU LIKE BEING THE PERSON YOU
ARE NOW, NEITHER DESPISE NOR
REGRET ANYTHING THAT GOT YOU
THERE.

Mistakes are part of human experience, whether we like it or not. Ideally, we learn from them and grow because of them. Making mistakes is not the problem. The real problem is the inability to adjust to mistakes. Maturity is the ability to adjust when we make mistakes.

Every individual could find things that he or she would change, given the opportunity to live life over again. This is very natural. In moments of weakness, we do things that we later recognize to be wrong. In moments of mindlessness, we say things that we wish we could take back. No one can repeat life or go back and undo the past. We can only learn to live with it.

It is impossible to appreciate the person you are now if at the same time you despise those things that have shaped you. Whether you like it or not, even your mistakes (large or small) are a necessary part of the building blocks that made you who you are. In fact, you could not possibly be the person you now are were it not for your mistakes.

We waste so much time living in the past. Looking

back is as fatal for us as it was for Lot's wife, who disobeyed God's command and, by looking back, was turned into a pillar of salt.

There is only one proper attitude about the past. Learn from it, but do not be controlled by it.

Christ taught that self-love is a very proper thing. His teaching illustrates the difference between Christ and the philosophy that historic Christianity has forced upon us. Some people believe that as good Christians they must love others but not themselves.

The truth of the matter is that you cannot love others until you love yourself. You cannot think well of others until you think well of yourself. You cannot accept others until you accept yourself.

As Jesus put it, only if you learn to love yourself will you be able to love others. A very necessary part of loving yourself is the ability to forgive yourself for anything and everything.

The central message of all Christianity is the message of forgiveness. God has forgiven everything. Now you must do the same. Stop living in the past. Stop trying to undo the unwise decisions of yesterday. Come to grips with all of your past and do the only rational thing that you can do, which is the same thing that God has done—forgive and forget.

I repeat the previously stated truth:

IF YOU LIKE BEING THE PERSON YOU ARE NOW, NEITHER DESPISE NOR REGRET ANYTHING THAT GOT YOU THERE.

In the eyes of God, you are worth a great deal. This theme is repeated throughout the Bible from the first chapter of Genesis on. Spirituality requires that you accept this as true of yourself.

Giving yourself attention is not unspiritual, rather it is part of spiritual growth. You have to know where you are before you can know how to get where you should be. In short, you must take time for yourself.

Time spent on yourself—on your own improvement, on developing your own potential—is time well invested.

The world around you sees God through you. If what they see in you turns them off, they will not stay around long enough to see God.

You should make the effort to be as attractive as possible. People who neglect their personal appearance are not honoring God. Your body is the temple of the Holy Spirit, and He deserves an appropriate dwelling.

Ask yourself about the quality of witness that you are making to the world. Money spent on self-improvement, the hairdresser's or barber's, on good clothes, on a good education—in short, anything spent on improving your image before the world, is money wisely invested.

It is spiritual to use your money for such personal needs as vacations, good automobiles or homes, because that is why God has blessed you with money in the first place.

There is a basic spiritual law that teaches us that those who work for things have a right to enjoy good things. In fact, you have a right to the best things in life. This is referred to as "the law of investment." It teaches that if you want to get something out of life, you must have already put something into it. Conversely, the person who has done nothing to help himself or to change his circumstance, who has put nothing into life, cannot expect to get anything out of life.

If you have been blessed according to the law of investment, then accept these things as blessings from God and use them as tools in your life. Mediocrity is a poor witness for anything.

Take time for yourself—no matter how busy your schedule. God has given you blessings as personal tokens of his love. Accept them with thanksgiving.

Part of learning to love yourself is the ability to take care of yourself and to do things for yourself. Self-neglect is not a spiritual doctrine. Self-stewardship certainly is. Once you have learned to love yourself, you will then be more able to love others. When you learn to love others, then you will want to share with them the blessings that you have received. There is ample evidence that blessings selfishly kept to ourselves seem to go bad, while blessings that are allowed to spill over on others are constantly being replaced.

Take time to do something that you enjoy. Take a trip that you have wanted to take for years, begin a new hobby, start a new program of training, join a club. Allow yourself the things you have previously labeled luxuries.

Usually when people are unable to do such things, they have an attitude problem concerning money. Some people believe that money is evil or at least that it is unspiritual. Such an attitude will keep a person in poverty because it is contrary to the spiritual law of blessing.

MONEY, PER SE, IS NEITHER GOOD
NOR BAD, BUT THE ABSENCE OF

## MONEY IS CERTAINLY EVIL AND
## CONTRARY TO THE WILL OF GOD.

In Psalm 1, the psalmist rejoices that the man who delights in God "shall be like a tree planted by the rivers of water, that bringeth forth his fruit in his season; his leaf also shall not wither, *and whatsoever he doeth shall prosper.*" The blessing of God brings prosperity and peace—bountiful harvests including money to pay your bills, fill your obligations, and help others. The absence of money is evil, because you can't pay your bills, take care of your family, or handle your obligations, and you have nothing left with which to help others. To the psalmist, the absence of money was synonymous with the absence of a blessing from God, because it denies us the necessities of life. So if you are trying to decide if money is good or bad, the reasoning is very simple. Money has to be good, because the absence of money is bad.

Take time for yourself—do something for yourself—spend money on yourself—all of these are paths to self-love and spiritual growth. The inability to do these things is indicative of too little self-acceptance and spiritual enlightenment.

In a later chapter we will more fully explore the spiritual laws concerning money, but for now, realize that you are worth a great deal more than you have previously believed.

If God sent so many blessings to tell you what he thinks of you, then you are worth a lot to him. Start believing it about yourself. You deserve the good things in life.

By God, you can do it.

# CHAPTER 15

# *Run Your Body or Your Body Will Run You—Ragged*

$A$sk yourself this question:

Does my body run me, or do I run my body?

A positive mind/body relationship is pivotal to our success in life. The best estimates that we can make from the Scriptures reveal that Jesus Christ spent about two-thirds of his ministry healing people. This ought to tell us something very important. God does not will illness upon us.

The accepted philosophy at the time of Christ was that God punished sin through illness or accidents. Unfortunately, this idea has survived, and many people still believe it.

I will never forget the mother that had just delivered a retarded infant. During my visit she asked me, "What great sin have I committed that God is punishing me in this way?" Her grief was so great I doubt if my answer was heard at that time.

There are several observations that can be made from the ministry of Jesus Christ.

1. Sickness is never the will of God;
2. Sickness is evil rather than spiritual;
3. God never sends illness as a punishment;
4. The right use of a faith overcomes any problem.

It cannot be denied that illness saturates our world. But God is not the author of illness, nor does He send it to anyone. Can the sun radiate darkness?

God is love, wholeness, and perfection. Doubtless He is much more, but He is at least that much. Love, wholeness, and perfection can never be the source of hatred, unwholeness, or illness.

Among the spiritual misconceptions that we have inherited is the principle of surrendering ourselves to our circumstances regardless of what they are. It may be easy for the person who lives a happy affluent life to accept that fatalist philosophy, but how about the bedridden, the crippled, or even the lonely. This belief perverts itself to the point that we doubt our spirituality if we murmur or complain about anything.

There is a basic truth that practically screams to us from the ministry of Jesus, and that truth is

IF YOU DON'T LIKE THE LIFE YOU
ARE LIVING, CHANGE IT. BY GOD,
YOU CAN DO IT.

Jesus Christ invariably rewarded the people who came to him for healing. He never said that spirituality was acquired through suffering. Not only did he deny that suffering was the will of God, he said that suffering was evil. He never denied anyone healing. In fact he proclaimed that illness, sickness, and suffering prevented people from living the full life that God has for them.

In John 5, Jesus stopped by the pool of Bethesda to heal a man who had been sick for thirty-eight years. Jesus first asked him if he wanted to be healed. We cannot infer from this question that people are sick because they want to be sick, but we can certainly infer that a person cannot be healthy unless he or she desires to be healthy. The man answered Christ by making excuses for his illness and pointing out that he had no one to help him. In other words he was blaming his illness on others. We still do that by blaming our illnesses on our families, our doctors, our employers, or somebody else. Remember that spirituality is not found by blaming others for your problems, but by confronting the problem and finding a solution. Jesus said to the man, you don't have to be here—you don't need this illness. Go on—get up and get out of here. The King James version is more polished: Jesus says, "Rise, take up thy bed, and walk." The man got the message and was healed. He left his illness behind because, at the invitation of Christ, he was determined to do something for himself. He could have refused his healing and stayed there, but he seized the opportunity to change his circumstances.

There is a basic relationship between you and your body. You, the spirit within your body, the true "you," is higher and more important than your body. Your body is your servant, designed by God to obey you and carry out your orders. You have the right to tell your body what to do. If you are unable to do this, there will be a mutiny and your body will run you.

In these last twenty years, we have been blessed with the science of biofeedback. Originally this was a discovery of scientists working in space programs. They discovered that mental control could regulate blood pressure, heart and breathing rate and even raise or lower the temperature in parts of the body. These and other discoveries verify the servant/master relationship between the body and the mind.

Now biofeedback has been moved into the counseling center and physical therapy clinics, where the marvelous powers that God has placed in the mind can be utilized as God meant for them to be.

To illustrate, let's examine what happens when a person gets a negative report from a doctor. The doctor may say to the patient who has suffered a disabling illness or injury, "You are going to have to learn to live with this." Immediately he surrenders to the condition. The arm that was disabled by a stroke hangs lifelessly by his side. The arthritic joint is immobilized or he limps along on it. If it's a heart condition, he confines himself to invalidism. If it's cancer, he asks how long he has to live.

The message of Jesus Christ is as relevant in the twentieth century as it was in the first century. If you have faith, you can overcome any illness or injury. Rather than surrender to your circumstances, you can rise above them. It is spiritual to conquer your circumstances, and it is wrong to surrender to them needlessly.

There are those experiences that are irreversible, such as the loss of a limb. But even here, rather than surrender to invalidism, we adjust to a new life-style and continue living in the fullest sense of the word. Faith has tremendous impact on life. It makes us more than conquerors, so it certainly makes us more than conquered.

## FAITH TURNS TRAGEDY INTO TRIUMPH.

The pages of the Bible are filled with stories about people who were touched by the power of God and healed of illnesses, diseases, and similar problems. The literature of the twentieth century describes the same types of healing. It is true—people are healed through the power of prayer and faith. The secret is found in the words of Jesus Christ: "According to your faith be it unto you" (Matt. 9:29). If you think God wants you to be sick, you will be sick—not because God wills it, but because YOU will it. On the other hand, if you think God wants you to be whole, it will be so because you will it.

The message of the Bible, combined with the best medical science of the twentieth century, tells us that we can rise above any circumstance, overcome any illness, and turn any tragedy into victory.

When you receive a negative prognosis, remember that it is what medical science expects in the average circumstance. But you are not to be average. You are a child of God, and deserve the best. The power that is available to you is the power of God. You are left not just to your own resources, because the resources of God are available to you. Use them for your victory.

When given a negative prognosis, accept it as being true for the present but reject it as being true of the future. This is an excellent time for imaging. Hold a mental picture of that arm working properly. Visualize the malfunctioning part of your body as becoming better and better. Literally will your wholeness. Reject any long-term disability. Work, pray, and trust God for the full utilization of the affected part or parts of your body according to the original and perfect plan of God. Accept nothing less as the will of God for you. If you pray for it and work for it, you can overcome any problem.

Instead of surrendering to your circumstances and resigning yourself to something less than a full life, rise above them. The will of God for you is your perfection, and it is worth fighting for. You are worth fighting for. Claim the victory through faith and action.

The power of God can overcome any illness, including cancer. Prayers are answered. Miracles do occur. There have been too many cases of healing for us not to believe this. Medical records are full of cases where cancers have been cured. Some doctors even specialize in the combination of medical therapy and meditation to combat tumors or other malignancies.

Too often, when cancer is diagnosed, the patient simply lies down and dies. Many people are dying of cancer who could live—who could overcome the illness if they had seen the doctor sooner, if they had accepted the best medical advice, and if they really believed that there was an alternative to death.

DYING, LIKE LIVING, IS A STATE OF MIND, AND EVERY DOCTOR HAS SEEN PEOPLE LIVE WHO SHOULD HAVE DIED AND PEOPLE DIE WHO SHOULD HAVE LIVED. "ACCORDING TO YOUR FAITH BE IT UNTO YOU."

I remember well the young boy of eleven who was brought to a prayer service. The doctors at one of the leading medical institutions of America had given him six months to live. He had cancer. The combination of their medical treatment, the loving support of his parents, the power of prayer, the power of God—all combined to cure his illness. Now he is in his thirties and living a normal life.

To be very honest about it—we do not know why people get sick, and we certainly cannot say why people get well. Why does illness touch one person and not another? Why does one person die and another person with a worse case recover?

Among all the confusion, one thing is very clear. The person who lives life in a happy relationship with God, who believes in himself or herself as a child of God, and who believes that a loving Heavenly Father sends only the best to his children will live a better life than the person who lives in fear and doubt.

Use these affirmations every day to aid you in running your body.

1. I am a child of God, and my Father loves and cares for me.

2. God sends me nothing but love and those things that can bless and fulfill me.

3. I reject all illness and disability as being contrary to God's perfect will for me.

4. I accept into my life only those circumstances that will fulfill God's perfect plan for me.

5. I surrender myself only to my Lord and to nothing that will detract from that perfect plan.

6. I am constantly energized by the power of God, and I share His health and wholeness.

Run your body, or your body will run you.

By God, you can do it.

# CHAPTER 16

# *Overcoming Handicaps*

*T*he dictionary defines a handicap as "a disadvantage that makes progress or success more difficult." Notice that it says nothing of an inability to perform but only that a handicap makes something "more difficult."

We often accept a handicap as a reason for not doing something. When a person is handicapped, we automatically assume that this person cannot do what others do.

All types of excuses are offered to explain a lack of progress. One person says he is handicapped by not having a good education. Another is handicapped by coming from a poor family or from the wrong part of town. Others feel handicapped by race, lack of money, age, or sex. The handicaps in life seem limitless, and they have something very significant in common.

Claiming that a handicap is responsible for a set of circumstances relieves us of responsibility and makes our problems seem unsolvable. Because of this, having a handicap frequently means suffering with "something we can never overcome."

Ironically it turns out that our greatest handicap is our inability to handle handicaps. Our feeling about the handicap, not the handicap itself, is the real crippler.

The concept of a handicap is relative. Many people who are regarded by others as handicapped do not consider themselves handicapped. They feel that the thing lacking is compensated for by other abilities. It is often the case that the loss of one physical sense strengthens the other senses. I know of a blind person with extremely acute hearing who refers to others who lack his ability to hear as being handicapped. Like beauty, handicaps exist in the eye of the beholder.

In the preceding chapter we offered an analogy— the relationship between you and your body is the same as the relationship between an employer and his servant. The servant obeys the master—and your body should obey you. You run it—if it runs you, then God's design is not being fulfilled.

Any circumstance is viewed as a handicap only if you accept it as such. Fill your mind with an inability or a disability, let fear rule your life, be preoccupied with what you can't do rather than what you can do, and you will be thwarted by these adopted handicaps. The potential that God has put within you will indeed be beyond your reach.

Persistence is critical to overcoming any barrier a handicap may seem to impose. It is the ability to stay at something until you have succeeded in your quest. Persistence means not giving up until you have reached your goal.

Suppose that you have suffered a broken limb or a

crippling stroke, and you pamper that part of your body by denying it the therapeutic value of exercise because pain is involved. The resultant handicap becomes one of your own creation—one that persistence could overcome.

Even in prayer we need to learn persistence.

We pray for something, and if it is not answered after a few prayers, we simply forget about it. God will never take seriously that which you do not take seriously. If you really want to see prayer work, do more than play at it. Be persistent in your prayers.

New Year resolutions, programs of self-control and discipline, additional training or education, new hobbies or life-styles—all of these things will work only when you are persistent.

> THE WAY TO HANDLE ANY
> HANDICAP, REGARDLESS OF
> WHAT IT IS, IS TO LAY OUT A
> PROGRAM THAT WILL OVERCOME
> THE PROBLEM AND THEN TO SEE
> THAT PROGRAM THROUGH
> TO COM PLETION. THIS IS
> NECESSARY WHETHER THE
> SO-CALLED HANDICAP IS
> EMOTIONAL, PHYSICAL,
> OR SOCIETAL.

No problem is ever solved by running from it. Whatever is holding you back from what God created you to be is a handicap that must be overcome, or you will find life both dissapointing and frustrating.

The best definition of a handicap is simply this:

anything that keeps you from being what you can be in God.

Maybe your handicap is an inability to speak in public, or perhaps you cannot function in a group. Maybe your handicap is a physical impairment. Regardless of what it may be, there is a solution that will lift you above it to successful living in God. But you must make the plan, in concert with the best advice from others, and then be persistent in carrying out that plan.

Over the last thirty years, we have been blessed with great advances in physical therapy. The therapist knows that pain is often necessary in overcoming a physical disability. Those of us who have suffered crippling injuries or illnesses often experience great pain in therapy programs, but the pain is never the real issue. We make it an issue by being preoccupied with the comfort/pain ratio. But if we are genuinely interested in restoring a dysfunction, then we must put our consciousness of pain aside and work toward the real goal—the restoration and refinement of our abilities.

In another chapter we discussed the concept of imaging. This power can be utilized to overcome our handicaps. Make a mental picture of overcoming the particular problem and keep that picture before you. See yourself doing what you are now unable to do. If you want to be a public speaker, visualize yourself talking to a large group. If you want to restore an impaired arm or leg, envision yourself walking or using that limb with no difficulty of any kind. If you desire to lose weight or build your physical image in some other way, visualize yourself as you would like to be.

Then work diligently until you are what you desire

to be. One of the best understandings of mental health is the reduction to zero of any conflict between what you are and what you desire to be. Frustrated people are not happy people.

Overcoming a handicap is hard work. For some people it might involve a lifetime of effort. Others may never successfully fulfill their goal. Others may overcome their handicap in a relatively short period. But you will never be able to conquer a handicap without persistence. There are no "quick fixes" to most human problems, and no one but you can solve your problems.

Persistence is really just another name for discipline. The disciplined person will carry out whatever project is important. Discipline and persistence are prime components of spirituality. Undisciplined people cannot be spiritual, and spiritual people discipline themselves with God's help.

Patience is also another necessary virtue. We take years getting ourselves into undesirable circumstances and then we expect God, others, or ourselves to solve them overnight. It is a general rule of life that what has been difficult over a period of time cannot be solved overnight. Marriages that degenerated over years cannot get a "quick fix" over a weekend.

Patience will help us to be persistent when we do not realize the immediate changes that we expect. Sometimes we examine our progress too closely. We do not see the change "right now," and so we decide there has been none. When we climb a mountain, we don't always realize how far we have gone until we look back to where we started. Then the contrast will be clearly seen.

Keep this thought before you.

I am not fully satisfied with what I am, and
I know I am not what I shall someday be,
but thank God, I am not what or where I
used to be.

Planning, persistence, and patience are never
enough. No handicap will ever be overcome without
activity on your part. You have got to be involved by
doing something. No one, not even God, will do for
you what you refuse to do for yourself.

Our large problems must be handled one step at a
time and one day at a time. You climb a mountain by
methodically putting one foot ahead of the other. Part
of the exuberance of climbing the mountain is the tired
muscles, the aching joints, the sometimes bruised
body—and the sense that each step you take is clearly
bringing you closer to your goal.

If you have a mountain of a handicap to climb, don't
be overwhelmed looking at the peak and thus resign
yourself to failure. Instead, take the first step and then
the second, and on until you have conquered that
mountain.

You are not alone. The loving Father that created
you knows every problem you face. God is involved
in helping you solve anything that is a problem to you.
He has not left you alone. He will work with you,
sharing His faith, His energy, and His success.

A little song says,

Got any rivers you think are uncrossable?
Got any mountains you can't tunnel
    through?

God specializes in things thought impossible
And He can do what no other power can
do.

Overcome all your handicaps.
By God, you can do it.

CHAPTER 17

# *You Are Spirit*

Several decades ago it was the accepted belief that every individual could be evenly divided up into three segments—body, mind, and spirit. Each segment was thought to be absolutely distinct, with no overlap of any kind. You went to the medical doctor for your body, to the educator for your mind, and to the clergyman for your spiritual needs.

One of the benefits of modern insight is that we now recognize that each person exists as a whole—an entity that blends physical, mental and spiritual needs. Holistic health is the modern approach to treating the whole person.

You can't have a sick mind without your body becoming sick sooner or later. By the same token, if your body is constantly sick, the effect on the rest of you can be devastating. And if your sickness is of the spirit, all of life will be drastically affected.

According to the best medical knowledge today, between eighty and ninety percent of all physical illness originates from the emotions. There are three times as many psychiatric beds in American hospitals as there are beds for those being treated for physical problems.

It is important to understand the basic compositions of your own life. The emotions play a more important role in a successful life than physical abilities do. It is easy to see that your emotional health is basic to your health in every way. Formerly it was thought that a healthy body made a healthy person. Now we know that emotional health is just as important as physical health. In fact, if your emotions are healthy, you can endure any temporary physical condition without suffering long-term damage. But if your emotions are ill, everything about you will be jeopardized.

It is also important to realize that your spiritual needs are not a separate area but that your spirit permeates every other dimension of your life. Some spiritual needs apply to your body and other spiritual needs apply to your mind and still different spiritual needs apply to your emotions.

The confusion caused by the old belief of the body/mind/spirit separation completely ignored the spiritual basis of all life. You are not a body that has a spirit and a mind. Rather you are a spirit temporarily encased in a body. The mind and the emotions belong to spirit, and temporarily they are expressing themselves through the physical being. Your mind acts through the computer we call the brain, and your emotions act through that mystic quality we refer to as soul. The soul is the common point of the spiritual and the physical, but it is basically emotional. The musical conductor, displeased by the performance of one or more of his musicians in rehearsal, may say to them, "Have you no soul?"

Let me illustrate with two drawings:

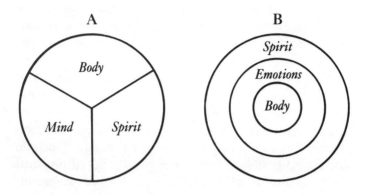

A is the old belief that we are composed of three equal and separate dimensions.

B illustrates the belief that each person is basically a spirit who has both emotions and a body, but they are not separate and distinct entities. The mind belongs to spirit and for now works through the brain. After physical death, you lose your body, but as spirit you still possess both mind and emotions.

On the spiritual level there is a real you (the spirit) that is just as real as your body is on the physical level.

It is not the purpose of this book to further explore the nature of spirit, but the preceding analysis is necessary to understand the concept of wholeness and the importance of treating the emotions and the body during sickness.

Many physically ill people have suffered a prior spiritual or emotional trauma.

Medical records are full of cases where traumatic incidents such as the death of a spouse, retirement, the loss of a job, or divorce are followed by terminal cancer. In most cases there was no prior record of a malignancy.

Self-pity is the frequent culprit that triggers the problem. Such an attitude contributes to the feeling of loss and adds a powerful negative influence over life.

The growth of counseling, both in the church and other clinical situations, reveals the basic emotional needs of the twentieth century. The need for counseling really grew out of the medical profession, when doctors began treating the emotional needs of people and found that such treatment often relieved physical illness—thus precipitating the practice of psychosomatic medicine. But all medical practice should treat the psyche (mind) as well as the soma (body).

Let's return to the problem of guilt. Much illness can be traced directly to a conscious and sometimes unconscious preoccupation with guilt. Here the church is most needed. If the message of spirituality is forgiveness, then the church needs to relieve people of guilt rather than instill it. Constantly reminding people that they are sinners will produce both continued sin and subsequent guilt. That guilt will lead to further emotional conflict and trauma, manifesting itself in physical illness or social dysfunction.

The Pharisees, who were the religious leaders of Jesus' day, objected to his teachings. While they focused on the law and punishment for sins, Jesus aimed to restore people to wholeness through the forgiving of sins. Strangely enough, we still see evidence of Phariseelike thinking in some twentieth-century clergymen. Psychologists and psychiatrists, who work to relieve people of their guilt and help them lead full lives, are following the precepts of Jesus Christ more closely than those clergymen who carp on guilt and punishment, making spiritual cripples of many who come under their influence.

Just as guilt binds and incapacitates, love, the greatest healing force in the world, liberates and empowers. The cure for guilt is the love of God working through self love and then a love for others.

Further evidence proves that you are a spiritual being. The things that mean the most to you are truly spiritual. You could live in a world without cars, airplanes, and washing machines, because people did so for thousands of years. But no one would want to live in a world lacking beauty, justice, goodness, and love. The quality of life would be empty and meaningless. All of these spiritual characteristics explain why simple physical living alone will never satisfy the inner yearnings of spirit.

Your basic composition is spiritual, because you have been created by God, the ultimate spiritual being. Into you He built a spiritual orientation that demands satisfaction in life. Mere material things will never satisfy that craving.

Every individual has basic spiritual needs, but that does not mean that every individual will satisfy them with religion. Man constructed religion to satisfy his spiritual orientation. But because religion is man-made, it ends up only playing games with our spiritual needs. Some of these games deal with the pride and exclusiveness that some religions foster in their followers. Others deal with arbitrary and very finite goals and then decree how to accomplish these goals. Some religions are obsessed with holy wars and the annihilation of those who are enemies of God. Sooner or later the spiritual mind realizes this and cries out for Spirit—

for God. Thus the spiritual mind leaves sterile religions behind and comes to God, just as the learning mind realizes the difference between "two plus two" and the concept of infinity.

There is no true satisfaction in life without the realization of our basic spiritual orientation. Success in life through business, politics, or other power pursuits will never satisfy the inner longings of the heart. Only God can do that.

Because you are spirit, you crave Ultimate Spirit. Fortunately, Ultimate Spirit (God) desires fellowship with you. He has even offered a daily, creative, personal relationship to you. It is not blasphemous to say that God wants and needs you as much as you want and need Him.

The greatest force in the entire world is that spiritual combination of an open life and an empowering God. This was the force behind many men and women who have graced the pages of history. Spiritual people have greatly advanced the causes of mankind. In contrast, religious people have often inhibited the advance of mankind. No greater anomaly exists in the entire world than so-called religious people killing each other in the name of God. But no greater spirituality exists anywhere in the world than the spirituality that seeks to relieve suffering and illness, pain and tragedy, defeat and despair and, in doing so, advances the well-being of mankind. That's what God is doing and spiritual people will always be involved.

If you have tried religion and have been disappointed—try God. If you have succeeded in life but failed miserably in your personal life—try God. If the road of life has had more bumps than blessings—try God.

You can do far more through and with God than you can ever do in any other way.

Life is good when lived as a spiritual experience. That is where success is.

By God, you can do it.

# CHAPTER 18

# *How to Handle Depression*

*D*epression is a reality that sooner or later touches every life. Everyone gets depressed about something at some point in life, and many people suffer from chronic depression. It seems that the more affluent we become as a society, the greater the risk of depression. This is because the depressed person must have time to be depressed—time when the mind is not consciously concerned about another problem. During that free time, self-pity, combined with a genuinely bad self-image, seems to overrule the mind and other emotions. Often the individual is in a state of dysfunction, not able to face others, particularly those who tend to be hypercritical.

We must guard against taking too simplistic a view of depression. Too often laymen, and occasionally even doctors, group all depressions into one type with one cause. The causes of depression may be manifold. Some depression is caused by a chemical imbalance in the patient. Severely depressed people must be clinically treated and have the best medical assistance available. However, the vast majority of depression seems to stem from an emotional malfunction or dysfunction and seems to be amenable to corrective techniques at less than a clinical level. It is to this sort that this chapter is mainly addressed.

I remember ministering to the wife of a rather affluent businessman. She had a fine house and several servants to do her work. Her problem was that she had never become involved in anything after raising the family. Consequently she had a great deal of time to sit around and think. Over the course of several years, she lapsed into a severe depression, requiring care by doctors, psychiatrists, and periods of hospitalization. Her case seemed to be without remedy. Strangely enough the situation took a dramatic reversal when her husband suffered a heart attack. The care of her husband during his illness gave her a new goal. Overnight all the depression disappeared, and she became the loving, solicitous person that she had been years before. She was instrumental in her husband's quick recovery, and they both learned valuable lessons. As a result of the crisis, they began to give each other more attention than any time previously in their marriage. The husband gave some of his business responsibility to subordinates, and he and his wife shared more activities. The wife realized that her depression had been an adopted attitude and never again afforded herself the crippling "luxury" of self-pity and dysfunction.

One of the most basic insights into mental health is

the fact that attitudes are adopted. We are not born with fear, feelings of inferiority or superiority, prejudice of any kind, self-esteem or self-denigration, or any other attitude. Some attitudes may be programmed into us as children, but even these are subject to later rejection as the mind develops a maturity of its own.

You are born with the unspoiled opportunity to fulfill the potential that the loving Creator has put within you. The only power in the world that can keep you from being the person you can be is you! No one but you can thwart—or develop—your own potential. The attitudes you adopt about yourself, life, and others will help determine your mental health.

In a very real sense depression and faith contradict one another. To understand this, let's examine faith.

Your faith, contrary to common consensus, is not where you go to church or what you believe about certain theological propositions. Faith is a dynamic force that begins with your attitude toward yourself, life, and the world in which you live. Faith is power— the power to remove mountains, as Jesus referred to it. It is a contagious, vibrant, positive attitude that looks at life and says, "No matter what you send my way, I can handle it."

The person whose life is full of faith is on the offense; he or she is taking charge of life, making decisions, and making things happen. The opposite of this is the person who exists as a doormat for others to use or abuse. This person has no say about his or her own destiny and simply takes what life hands out.

Let's make some comparisons between faith and depression:

| *Faith* | *Depression* |
|---|---|
| 1. The ability to do | 1. The inability to do |
| 2. Self-esteem | 2. Self-denigration |
| 3. The ability to face people | 3. The inability to face people |
| 4. Eagerness to start the day | 4. Trepidation to begin the day |
| 5. Jumping out of bed | 5. Hiding under the covers |
| 6. Looking to the future | 6. Living in the past |
| 7. The ability to dream | 7. Lack of vision |
| 8. Zest for living | 8. Lack of motivation |
| 9. Maturity | 9. Immaturity |
| 10. Finishing your tasks | 10. Dropping projects in the middle |

The list could be expanded but these are enough descriptions to show that faith is the opposite of depression.

Since most of this book addresses the idea of faith, let's now devote our attention to handling depression.

1. Depression is a reaction to certain pressures that you find discomforting in life. It can cause you to withdraw into a protective nook. But note that this is an attitude you adopt. No one forces it upon you. No one outside of you can make you depressed. We tend to blame our depression on others but that is part of our immaturity and the inability to adjust to stress. We say, "My boss depressed me," when what we really should say is, "There was a confrontation at the office and being unable to handle the pressure, I allowed myself to lapse into self-pity and depression." If we

had the maturity to make that kind of analysis, the resultant depression would be very short-lived.

Because depression is an attitude to which we succumb, part of the remedy is to adopt the opposite attitude, namely the attitude that "By God, I can overcome any problem, any confrontation, and I will be the victor in life and not the victim."

When we fill our lives with positive faith, depression has no room in which to flourish. If you have had problems with depression, program yourself with positive ideas of your own worth and your own abilities. Repeat affirmations over and over to yourself until the unconscious mind begins to believe them and incorporates them into everyday living. Force yourself to do these things and depression will no longer run your life.

2. People who are depressed often find they cannot function. They are unable to do things such as go to work, face others, finish their tasks, etc. The secret of overcoming inaction is action. Force yourself to do things. Force yourself to solve your problems. Force yourself to face others. Force yourself to finish your tasks.

We are creatures of habit. Almost everything you do is simply a habit. Eating three or more meals a day is a habit. Snacking is a habit. Going to bed each night at 10 PM or getting up each morning at a certain hour is a habit. Smoking is a habit. Excessive talking is a habit. The person in charge of his or her life is not ruled by habits. Rather he or she commands the habits and uses them as spices are used in cooking, that is, to add flavor to life.

The best time to ward off depression is in the earliest stage—not after it becomes a habit. Once you start feeling the formation of self-pity and withdrawal, nip it in the bud. Refuse to allow that weed to ruin the garden of your life. Do things and keep doing them until the unconscious mind has been reoriented away from self-pity.

Keep your mind busy and your body active, and there will be no room for depression. Inactivity and withdrawal are malignancies that lead to even worse problems.

3. Usually depressed people are not well organized. Well-organized people are productive people who stick to a schedule and finish assignments. That is why successful people are the ones who get things done. An old adage says that if you want a job done, give it to a busy person and it will be accomplished. On the other hand, people with time on their hands never have time to do anything. This irony emphasizes our previous comments on habits.

Another way to handle depression is to schedule your entire day for the most productive output. Keep a daily log of your appointments or responsibilities and then force yourself to adhere to the schedule. Time is money, and people who are careless with either will tend to be depressed. .

4. Another cure for depression is a genuine dose of self-esteem. People who are depressed often have a bad self-image. If you lack confidence in your own abilities, the cure is to find that confidence by working on projects or toward goals.

No one would ever be depressed if he really understood how much God thinks of him. If the One who knows all about you—even more than you know about yourself—thinks so highly of you and of your worth, then you ought to think more highly of yourself.

The authority on you is not you. You cannot possibly be objective. The authority on you is God, and you ought to listen to what He thinks of you.

When one surveys nearly two thousand years of church history in the Christian movement, probably the greatest consciousness that theologians have created is the consciousness of sin. That is a tragedy. How much greater would it have been if our minds were filled with the consciousness of God instead! Forget putting yourself down, forget your mistakes—think of yourself as a creation of the loving Father who daily wants to be in a partnership with you. God's love for you and the healing that power brings to life is itself enough to overcome your depression.

5. Sometimes people who are depressed need a change—they need to get away. Productive people usually know how to relax, but others may need a change of pace to break the habit of routine living. If you have previously been unable to give yourself attention or esteem, reverse that situation by taking time for yourself. Unwind with a night out. Have dinner and go to a movie or a play. Visit a museum or a historic place. Take a day off and just sleep late or do something else you would like to do. Maybe you need to do nothing but sleep and rest for a day. That is quite all right, as long as it deviates from an otherwise hectic routine and does not become a habit in itself. The basic idea is to recognize that you are the most important person in your life and you owe it to yourself to take care of you. If you don't take care of you, nobody else will.

Most people could handle their depression if they would follow the previous suggestions. Depression is not inescapable, but life is too wonderful to be spent in a depressed state.

Some special occasions may require professional attention such as the services of a minister, a psychiatrist, or a psychologist. Sometimes a depression can be too deep to climb out of on one's own.

One word of caution is needed here. No one but you can solve your depression. If you are simply trying to put your problems onto someone else, it won't work. Don't expect a professional to magically cure your depression without any effort on your part. Don't play games with your depression. Don't use it as a crutch in life.

Realize that depression is an adopted and crippling injury to all aspects of life and that you are far better off without it. You have the power to make the change. God has given you the ability to overcome all your problems.

The testimony is there.

By God, you can do it.

# CHAPTER 19

# How to Handle Negativity

*I*f you want to be a successful person living a fulfilled life, you must learn to overcome the negativity that will constantly confront you. For every good idea that you will have, there will be at least one negative person around to "enlighten" you about why your idea will not work. When you have great ideas, the negativity multiplies astronomically.

The choice between being negative and being positive is really the choice between being destructive and being creative. Anyone can destroy. In fact, some insecure, competitive people seem to delight in destroying the ideas of others. But being positive is being creative, and that takes far more effort and thought. Remember this saying:

ANYBODY CAN DESTROY, BUT ONLY POSITIVE PEOPLE CREATE.

Probably the greatest harm that anyone can ever do to another person is to make that person negative.

Children are particularly vulnerable to negative influences. There is no greater disservice that any parent can do to a young mind than to make that mind negative. We will never know how much intelligence has been lost by sincere but sincerely mistaken parents who stifle their children's ambitions telling them, "You aren't smart enough to do that." Dashed hopes may rise again, but young minds constantly pushed down by negative parents may never rise.

If you are a parent of a young child, your greatest responsibility is to help that young mind reach its potential. Encourage your child to "think big"— challenge him or her to dream, to excel rather than stifle that child's potential.

One reason that parents harbor negative attitudes toward their children's abilities is because the parents have poor self-images. If you think poorly of yourself, you will have a tendency to think poorly of all that you produce. "Look, it's my child—I know he is not too bright." All the time the parent is thinking, ". . . because I am not too bright."

Usually intelligent parents will produce intelligent children, but there have been cases where very average parents have borne child prodigies. A basic guideline to follow when dealing with a young and developing mind is: do everything that you can to fulfill that potential and do nothing to stifle it. This is a good rule to follow in all relationships, and it will make you a person others love to be around regardless of your age or their age.

Negativity is demonic. It rises from a negative life

and suffocates everything it touches. It is a truly insidious influence, yet some people take pride in it, pointing out how "realistic" they are. Being destructive is not realism—it is intellectual murder and suicide. Honesty requires that it be recognized as such.

When you develop an idea you think has potential, you have several means of protecting yourself from the destructive influence of negative people.

1. At first keep the idea to yourself. Think it through and test it in every possible way. That way you protect yourself from earning the reputation of "going off on hairbrained schemes." Sometimes the idea will be great, but you have not sufficiently thought it through before presenting it to others. That is fair neither to yourself nor your idea. Sometimes ideas need time to germinate before they are exposed to the hard light of examination. To test them prematurely is unwise. Furthermore, when you keep your ideas to yourself until they are sufficiently developed, you protect yourself from someone else stealing your idea and developing it as his own.

2. When it is ready, test your idea on successful people. Why discuss potential successes with people who have never known success? Their responses will be affected by their negative attitudes, and you don't need to hear that kind of response. People who have known success in life will encourage other visionaries, and the recurrent success will mutually benefit both partners. If you want your ideas to succeed, don't expose them to people who can't explore life fully. This is not an elitist attitude. Rather it is an honest appraisal as to where you can find help when you need it. Successful people are anxious to lift others. People who are not successful drag others down with them.

In all of life be very careful where you get your advice.

3. Believe in your idea in the face of criticism. Sometimes the critics are not testing the idea but are testing you. Maybe you are being considered for a promotion or a new job. Successful people admire others who believe in themselves and in their ideas. Many great ideas have become successful operations because the person who presented the idea had done his homework. His enthusiasm became the factor that swayed the decision. A man who doesn't believe in his own ideas does not believe in himself.

Let's discuss another type of negativity—medical negativity. We have touched upon this in previous chapters, but we need to look at it in this light also.

Some may question the phrase "medical negativity" and suspect that it shows an antimedical bias, but that certainly is not the intention here.

By medical negativity I mean any situation in which you are compared to some average circumstance and on the basis of the average a projection is made about your future and the quality of life you will have to live.

I have no arguments about medical statistics. They clearly reveal what we can expect as the average. But that is my point—the average does not necessarily apply to you.

The "average" to which statistics refer often does not even exist. As an example, the average American has two-and-one-half children, but I know no one who has two-and-one-half children.

When a doctor or a therapist says to you, "Here is what you can expect, in the light of your condition," he is simply drawing on the average circumstance of people who have gone through the same thing as you. But any time there is an average, there have to be people both above and below the average. If you surrender to those statistics, then your life-style will conform to the average. On the other hand, you may reject the statistics and determine not to be average. Declare that you are different, and you will beat the odds. If you genuinely believe this, the chances are great that you will do just that.

Sometimes the advice comes not from doctors but from friends. But remember—free advice is usually worth what you pay for it. People who have gone through similar operations or accidents can be very helpful as long as they have positive outlooks. Most large cities have lay groups to help others in post-surgical recuperation, and the results seem to benefit both parties. But the last thing that any person needs is some wet blanket who will give him a negative outlook about the value of continued living.

By God, you do not have to be average, and you can overcome most problems if you simply believe in yourself and believe that God is at work in you to help you overcome your problems. On the other hand, to give up is fatal.

Negativity often influences the career decisions that we make. Sometimes we have been preconditioned toward or against certain careers. For years, women were expected to be nurses if they had an interest in medicine because everyone knew that "Only men can be doctors." That reasoning was as inane as the reasoning that keeps women from becoming ordained in many churches today.

I know of a woman who was determined to have a

vocal career despite the fact that her early teachers told her that she was wasting both time and money. Yet she believed in herself, and she was determined to reach her goal. She developed a beautiful voice—not because she had some "gift," but rather because she was dedicated and worked hard to realize her own dream.

In most cases it is true that inspiration is ninety percent perspiration. People get what they work for. This also explains failure—strive to be nothing, and you will succeed.

Suppose the negativity around you is a "social negativity," that is, negativity of people that you meet in everyday life. Because this type is unsuspected, it might be the most insidious.

Here are some rules to protect you from negativity.

1. Protect yourself with a barrier of faith. In Ephesians 6 the apostle Paul said, "Take unto you the whole armour of God." You do not have to accept the negative darts of others, rather you can let them bounce off you.

If you protect yourself with a barrier of faith, you will be conscious of the negative people always around you, but you will reject their influence at the same time that you accept and love them as people.

Sometimes people are thoughtless and cruel. I have heard people say to someone else, "My, you look bad," and the person to whom they were speaking starts wondering if and why he looks bad and either gives in to an illness or invents one so as not to embarrass his friend. With friends like that, no one needs enemies.

Be selective. No matter what someone says to you,

whether it is about you or someone else, don't allow any negative idea to trap you. Be on the offense and full of faith. Reject negativity.

"You look like you're coming down with something," "You look like you're catching a cold," are statements that we ought not make one to another. Don't place negativity in someone's mind.

2. Be positive in your influence on others. Inspire people rather than discourage them. Share with them the ideas of God's goodness and love and that God wants to help them in all of their problems. If it is at all possible, encourage them to adopt for themselves a positive attitude about life.

I remember well a beautiful young lady who seemed to have been raised on negativity. Though she was working in her chosen career, life seemed to be passing her by. One day I took the risk of sitting down with her and talking about the wholesome influence of faith. She seemed to absorb some of the new thoughts I was presenting to her. A week later she came back to me with a beaming personality and a smiling face, and she said excitedly, "Reverend Kirkley, it works!" Not long after that she met a fine young man she later married, and now they have a happy home and a family—all because "it works."

3. You just can't change some people. Regardless of how they are, they have the right, and maybe the need, to be as they are until something happens to change them. Until that time, you may want to minimize your contact with them. Don't force yourself on them. Not everyone is ready for what you have. You don't have the right to invade their privacy. But at the same time, they don't have the right to invade your privacy.

Sometimes this problem is complicated because it

may involve a marital partner. Then your privacies overlap, but you can still minimize the negative influence by refusing to adopt attitudes or ideas that are alien to you. Maybe a good marital counselor is needed; if so, by all means use one.

The way to handle negativity is not to let it touch you. Be selective in your friends and the influences and ideas that you allow to touch your life. It is your life, and you must take care of it.

Paul gives very good advice in Romans 12:21:

> Be not overcome of evil, but overcome evil with good.

By God, you can do it.

# CHAPTER 20

# *Having the Right Attitude about Money*

*P*robably no area of your life reveals problems as clearly as your financial situation. It is the best barometer to warn you of impending storms.

The role of finances confuses most people, yet money is a crucial factor in the successful life.

The surplus or lack of money is not really the issue. The real issue is the attitude that we take toward our affluence or poverty and the reasons that we offer to explain our present circumstances.

It is a basic law of life that every person should have the resources that provide both necessities and pleasures.

Not all desires are the same. One person may like to travel, while another simply wants to improve his home or put money in the bank. Contentment, in this context, means the ability to do what you want to do.

It is wrong to want to do something just because someone else has done it. If your desires are always created by copying others, then you are not being your own person. You should have your own desires—desires that are drawn out of your own needs, likes, and dislikes. To want to take a cruise simply because your neighbor took a cruise and you don't want to fall behind in the race of one-upmanship is not good. The things that you do should be decided solely upon the basis of your own desires and needs.

The secret of success, in being able to do what you want to, often revolves around your attitudes. If you have a bad attitude about the role money should play in life, you are cutting the flow of money off from your life.

Let's examine some of the negative attitudes that people have about money.

1. "Money is evil, and I don't want anything to do with it." If you have this attitude, you cannot function well in modern society. People who adopt this attitude usually are underpaid if they work at all. Marital problems often spring from this attitude, whether or not both people share the same feeling. I have known wives who, looking upon money as something "not to be allowed around the house," made it impossibly difficult for their husbands to keep ahead of the bills. Sometimes the wife is held in poverty by a husband who condemns her craving for more money as being undisciplined. The driving force of this misconception seems to be that money will pollute you if it stays around too long—get rid of it as soon as you can.

2. Another negative attitude is that others may deserve money, but I don't—"I am not good enough to have the basic needs of life fulfilled." This is just another form of putting yourself down—"I haven't won anywhere else in life, why should I win here. I'm a loser—I will never get ahead."

3. Some people think that money is good only when used for others. They have guilt feelings if they spend anything on themselves. I have known parents who would deny themselves things so that they could spend what money was available on their children. Others feel that they must give their money to missionary causes or charities. Again self-image is the problem— "I don't deserve the good things of life."

4. The more insidious attitude is the one that says you can't be spiritual if you are concerned with money. Some religious systems enforce this view upon certain segments of their communities. Buddhist priests are not allowed to have money and must beg for their daily food and other needs. Some Christian orders require vows of poverty, insisting that their communicants renounce involvement with mercenary interests. The hypocrisy of such an attitude is revealed when others are expected to support these "spiritual people." Spirituality is never found through transferring your problem to someone else or by having someone else take care of you.

Certain concepts that apply to the use of money must be clearly understood.

1. Money is a medium of exchange, and as such is only good. However, as in much of life, that which is basically good can be misused for evil purposes. I can use my money to bribe an official, but the evil is in my intentions and not in the money.

We often hear the Bible misquoted to say "money is the root of all evil." That is not what the Bible says. The exact quote in 1 Timothy 6:10 in the King James version is "the love of money is the root of all evil." In that sense it is referring to avaricious greed. It is referring to the Scrooge who withholds just wages from his employees or the manipulator who uses money to enslave others. The abuse or misuse of anything is the evil and not the thing itself.

2. The creative flow of money is like a stream that both cleanses and refreshes that through which it flows. There is a divine law of creativity. As money flows through a business, it blesses those who are employed there, it enriches those who have invested in the business, and it helps those who purchase the product. Stop that creative flow, and every segment will suffer loss. If the workers demand all the benefit, the flow will stop. If those who operate the business insist on all the profits, the flow will stop. If the consumers demand that no one make a profit on them, the flow will stop. Communism cannot meet its own needs because it has hopelessly dammed the flow. This creative law is illustrated in all of life—the cycles of the seasons, the process of birth, life and death, learning and growing. Life is a flow, and creative resources must be kept in flow. What applies to business also applies to the business of running your life.

3. There is no shortage of money. There is always plenty of money around, but it may be that someone else has it and not you. Now the question becomes "How do I get my share?" and that is far different from the question "Is there enough money?" Nature is an abundance.

4. Your attitudes attract to you either money and success or poverty and failure. If you have been negative about the role and purpose of money in your life, you need to make a change. Adopt the attitude that you desire these blessings and that you are open to receive them. Life will not force money on you against your will. Successful people have learned the laws of

success, and thus they become blessed. Others stand around and envy those who succeed. This does not put them into the flow of blessing. In fact the bitterness that jealousy engenders is an even greater obstacle to becoming blessed in life.

5. Money and other blessings will flow to those who create the opportunity for being blessed and who open the door to blessings.

Because this is a spiritual universe, only those who work to receive their blessings will continue to be blessed. The mentality that says, "I am *your* problem," will never be blessed. Those who stand around with their hands out waiting for others to help them will never receive the help they truly need. As this book has repeatedly asserted—your problem will be solved only when you are dynamically involved in the solution.

6. The flow of money is a spiritual concept. Jesus said that it is more blessed to give than to receive. This is easy to understand. The person who receives is blessed only once, but the person who gives is blessed twice. He will be blessed by his giving to another, but he will be blessed a second time as life replaces the gift that he has given to another. When you give away something in your life, you are creating a space that needs to be filled. Life will bless you by the filling of that need. It is true about both giving and life: "Nature abhors a vacuum." When you share with others in love, you are creating a void that another blessing will fill. Thus it is more blessed to give than to receive.

With these six concepts in mind, let's discuss the ways that we can increase the flow of money and other blessings into our lives.

1. Rid yourself of the idea that money is evil and replace it with the concept that money is a good thing, and it is welcome *without limit* in your life. Remember that before you can have blessings, you must desire these blessings. But we must make it clear that we are doing this "without limit." We often make the mistake of figuring how much we need, and we open ourselves to just that amount. "I want ten thousand dollars to pay my bills" or "I only need fifty thousand dollars to purchase this home." What we are really saying is that anything over the specified amount is evil and it is not welcome in our lives. On the other hand, when we say that money is good and that we welcome it *without limit*, we make no such hypocritical limits, and we are opening our lives to being totally blessed. The blessed life has no room for hypocrisy.

2. Create the climate into which blessings can flow. Create a plan through which you can use your money. Plan to invest it, spend it, share it with others but invent a creative plan that will keep money in circulation. Blessings that are simply "hid in the mattress" soon self-destruct, while greed blocks the future flow of blessings.

3. Realize that there is no lack in nature, that there is sufficient blessing for all, and that it is the Father's will to give you the kingdom. As a child of God loved by the Father, you are worthy to be blessed and you will be blessed.

4. Go one step farther and declare through affirmations that all the blessings of life are flowing to you now and that you receive them graciously. Electrical current flows from the source to the need when the circuit is not blocked. The blessings of life will flow

from the source (God) to the need (your life) when the circuits are open.

5. Remember that God is the source of blessing and do not confuse the source of the blessing with the means of the blessing. You may think that your problems would be solved if your boss would give you a two-hundred-dollar raise. But that is to emphasize the means and not the source. Keep your attention on the source and do not dictate the means.

6. Share your blessings with others. Use a portion to help others who have not yet been as blessed as you are. The biblical standard was to give 10 percent. Some may give more and some may give less but all have to learn that not to give is to cut off the supply. When you give do it cheerfully. The Scripture says that God loves a cheerful giver (2 Cor. 9:7). This is because God himself is a cheerful giver, and when we emulate Him, we move closer to being like God. And our real goal in life is to be like Him.

7. Be sure that you are holding up your end of spiritual law. You can't expect to be blessed in life if you are not working to receive those blessings. Every person needs the stimulation of being gainfully employed in order to have self-esteem. Blessings cannot flow to the life that has a bad self-image. There is always something you can do to start the flow of money. You may have to move to find work or perhaps train for a new career,but do something, for not to be involved is fatal. If you sit back and wait, life will continue to pass you by. Don't let pride stand in the way.

Blessings without limit lie within reach, ready to be given by a loving Father who wishes to share with you all the good things of life. But to have these,

You must believe;
You must be open to receive;
You must be ready to use them; and
You must share them with others.

By God, you can do it.

CHAPTER 21

# *Take Time for Yourself*

$A$re you martyring yourself for a cause? Are you sacrificing yourself for the well-being of another? Are people constantly using you for a doormat to wipe their shoes on? Are you laboring for a husband, wife, or a family that doesn't appreciate you? If so, it's time to do something about it. No one but you can make things different. You have to take time for yourself.

Martyrdom and self-sacrifice are very misused and misunderstood concepts. They may fit very well with the guilt and self-denigration that society likes to force upon some of its members, but they will never qualify as things that people ought to willingly adopt.

To be brutally frank about it, people who force themselves to be martyrs and continually sacrifice themselves to the interests of others have problems that clearly need to be confronted. Self-martyrdom is the coward's suicide. It is surrendering your life to a situation that will destroy you. Self-sacrifice is always the by-product of a bad self-image. When you think properly about yourself, you do not put yourself second to any cause. Your life is more important than any external issue.

I do not doubt the sincerity of those who are continually belittling their value when compared to others, but the practice defies rationality. Never forget this basic truth; you are the most important person in your life. You must take care of yourself. If you don't you will not be around to help or take care of anyone else.

Some situations call for overextending yourself for a period of time. Classic examples are mothers with a sick or handicapped child, spouses who must take care of their marital partner, or those required to take care of a family member. No one however, should resign himself to such a way of life without recourse to relief.

Apart from these extended circumstances, surrendering personhood for the good of some other person or institution is a negative action. You are not a better person just because you give up your freedom for the good of some movement. In fact, you will probably be a poorer person for it. Not only are you using time and effort that could be more wisely spent, but you are surrendering yourself to a philosophy that denigrates you as a human being.

If you haven't learned this lesson before, learn it now:

THERE WILL ALWAYS BE PEOPLE
AROUND WHO WANT YOU TO DO
THEM A FAVOR AT YOUR EXPENSE.
SOME OF THESE PEOPLE ARE

SKILLFUL ENOUGH TO MAKE YOU
FEEL GUILTY IF YOU DON'T GO
ALONG WITH THEIR LITTLE PLAN.

Let's talk first about time.

Every person needs some free time when they can do whatever they want. This need is proportional to the strain of the situation you are in. The mother who has been home all day with sick children should be able to have free time at night after her husband comes home. She should be able to go out with friends, visit, go bowling, go to a movie, or do something else that she enjoys. But the choice is hers. The husband who has been hard at work all day should also find time to relax. He should not be met at the door with a list of "must" items.

If you divide the weekdays up into mornings, afternoons, and evenings, there are fifteen segments. Weekends are not taken into account. The average person should have at least one segment through the week when he or she can relax and escape from all other responsibilities. Maybe the husband and wife want to go out together, in which case a baby-sitter is in order. No matter what the choice, husbands and wives need to work together to provide "private time" for each other so that they can both be free to unwind.

Furthermore, both husbands and wives need time away, like an occasional weekend, where either one or both can take a trip if desired. Our society seems to frown on husbands or wives being on trips without their partner, but that is caused by insecurity. The man who gives his wife the freedom to visit with friends or just to go away alone will be rewarded with a more vibrant and appreciative partner. This is particularly true if the husband stays home to take care of the children, which is something the wife has been doing all week anyway.

Sometimes couples need to leave their children with others and go away alone for the weekend. This is ideal if both have been working all week. Sometimes parents carry guilt because they think they are neglecting their children, but an occasional weekend apart will benefit all the family relationships.

Within a family, it's common for members to take each other for granted. Unless attention is paid to this issue, it can become a problem. Husbands, wives, parents, and children should make time to appreciate one another by doing things together.

Also, take time for yourself—you need it, and you will be a better person because of it. In some situations, you may have to demand it, but you have that right, and no reasonable spouse will deny it.

Not only is it not immoral to take time for yourself, it is good common sense. You will be a better wife, husband, mother, or father because of the opportunity to get away from the pressure of daily living and relax in some situation of your own choosing. People who are constantly on the go will invariably suffer burnout or other stress problems.

Maybe the time you need to spend on yourself should be spent in an educational setting. Taking courses and studying can be a valuable, rewarding, and relaxing change of pace for most people. This may be particularly so if the course selected is in a field unrelated to your occupation. Maybe you need a hobby that will allow you freedom to unwind. Almost everyone has something that they would like to do if given the time to do it. Find it and do it.

You have all the time in the world—take time for yourself. You need it. You are worth it, and you will be a better person for it.

People who plan leisure time and are consistent in taking it will have fewer problems than those who do not.

Taking time for yourself also includes doing things for yourself. You can spend money on yourself without guilt as long as it is not an amount you cannot truly afford. It is not a matter of "robbing Peter to pay Paul" but rather a matter of figuring out how much of your family budget you have the right to spend on yourself. Just as you like your children to look well dressed, they have a right to a parent who is also well dressed. Feeling pride in one's appearance contributes to a sense of well-being. Your children will only benefit from your positive self-image.

When you spend time on yourself, you will take care of yourself in other ways, too.

You will discover that intellectual pursuits challenge your mind to grow. In utilizing all your talents, your potential will be realized. Study, learn, and grow— repeating that cycle over and over. Not to do so is to vegetate.

Along with your mind you will take care of your body. Remember, you should run your body. It should not run you. Taking time for yourself means taking time to be the person you want to be.

You are the most valuable person in your life. Although relationships with others are crucial, you must take ultimate responsibility for your life. Others may leave you or hurt you; life carries no guarantees. Ultimately, you are all you have. Take good care of yourself. Take the time to do so.

By God, you can do it.

CHAPTER 22

# *Putting It All Together*

*P*erhaps some of the concepts that I have presented in this book are so different that you
have had difficulty accepting them. There is, however,
a basic truth that I have learned to accept in life that
can be constructive for you:

TRUTH IS WHERE YOU FIND IT.

What we have covered in this book is the very sincere gleanings of a life that has sought to bring together
successful living impacted with all the spiritual power
that is contained in our universe.

At any given stage of a person's growth, only so
much newness can be tolerated. What you can accept
and use now is what you should accept and use now.
If something does not help you at this time, just put
it on the shelf for a while. Later on you may be able
to use it.

Three concepts stand out in this book:

1. Life will be what *you* make it;
2. All limitations are *self-imposed*;
3. God and the entire universe will help those who *help themselves*, but nothing can be done for the person who waits for someone else to solve his problems.

What you believe about yourself, the world, and God are fundamental to success in life. It may not seem so to you, but this is a good world, where those who rise to the top are those who have learned the laws of life.

Living is the most important task that faces you, but there is no school that can prepare you ahead of time. You learn the lessons of life in the school called life, and those who learn quickly and adapt survive.

The world does not pamper those who are weak. Not even nature does that. Those who are strong are those who survive; but the strength is of body, mind, and spirit.

The most important thing to remember is that when you believe in yourself, you are starting to tap the great reservoir of power that God has placed in you.

All the energy of the universe—all the power that you need for successful living—lies within you. You are an infinite gold mine of potential. Get rid of your inhibitions. Clear away the roadblocks. Sometimes it is necessary to get yourself out of the way so that the life smoldering within you may be released.

God holds no one back, and to blame your lack of progress on God or anyone else reveals your failure to confront the real issues of life. Everything that you need, God has given to you. Just start using the power that is within. You have to be a self-starter, because no one but you can turn you on.

More than we like to admit it, our circumstances

mirror for us the kind of people we are at any given stage of our development. Fear, sickness, poverty, frustration, and many other negatives are simply external reflections of internal turmoil. But you have the potential to control your circumstances, and if you do not use that potential, then the circumstances will control you. As in physical illness, the symptoms are not the source of the problem, but they give clues to the problem. To treat only the symptoms without treating the problem may bring temporary relief, but it cannot effect a long-range cure. Yet God has given you all the resources you need for a permanent cure.

Ideas are the answers to any problem in life. Behind every problem are ideas for solving it. This is the law of creation. Create an idea that will solve your problems, then use all of the remarkable powers of the mind and all the spiritual laws of life to devise the solution to the problem.

Law does run life. It determines success or failure, happiness or misery, health or disease, and all other contrasts in life. The secret is to find those laws that govern success and then have the dedication to follow through with them. Life respects law because life is law. Those who have not learned this relationship must sooner or later realize that failure always has a reason, for failure is the by-product of not learning the laws of success. An old business maxim says, "When you fail to plan, you plan to fail." People who have learned the laws of successful living can never be ultimately defeated, though they may have temporary setbacks, and people who fail to learn those laws cannot go on stumbling into success, because life respects its own laws too much to violate them.

Use the laws of life to make good things happen for

you. Why just sit back and take whatever life gives you when you can be in charge of life and make good things happen for you and others around you. The truly constructive person is one who helps himself and others. In fact, it would be immoral to refuse to help others if you had it in your powers to help them. Thus it seems that one definition of morality is the ability to help others discover a better life. When you make good things happen for yourself, and those around you, you are cooperating with the creative laws of the universe and therefore with the Creator.

God is on your side working with you for the successful life. The next greatest resource is yourself. You are your greatest ally if you use all of your abilities. If you do not, you may be your own worst enemy.

Because God has already accepted you, you can now accept yourself. Throw away guilt, feelings of inferiority, fear, and other burdens. The average person carries much excess baggage that holds him back.

There is a real you that is waiting to be released. Every day it is renewed, and its opportunities to flourish constantly increase. That is part of the God-inspired life. There is the thrill of being surprised by the next success and marveling at all that is accomplished. This kind of life can never be boring.

At this point throw away all of those negatives that hold you back: self-pity, guilt, fear of failure, fear of success, self-denigration, self-martyrdom, self-abuse— throw them away, because you don't need them. There are far greater resources available to you. Be clothed in the new you that God has for you each day.

Because there is a new you each day, you don't need those illnesses that you have accumulated over the years. You have the power to let them go; do it now.

When your mind is filled with the positive things of life, there will be neither time nor need for negative things.

Your body belongs to you—not vice versa. From this day on, make it quite clear that you are in charge and you will now be giving the orders. Remember that you have neither time nor the need for illness, so crowd the possibility right out of your life. The life that is closed to illness cannot become sick. Why be sick anyway? God does not want you to have illness and you don't need it. Simply reject both illness and the possibility of illness.

The true "you" is spirit. The body that you carry is only the house in which the spirit now resides. Your spirit reaches out for ultimate spirit (God). You will never find satisfaction in life unless and until you realize the spiritual basis of your existence. But that is what this book has been all about. All the laws of spirit are laws of success, and all the laws of success are laws of spirit. When your spirit is whole, all the rest of you will be whole, but there is no greater hunger in the entire world than the hunger of spirit.

Spirit always triumphs. That is the central theme of spiritual understanding. Because spirit triumphs, there need be no defeats, although we might endure temporary setbacks.

Depression, negativity, poverty, and similar problems need never touch the life in spirit, because we are protected by spiritual law and the creator of that law.

We started this book by saying that life will be what *you* make it. Only you hold true power over you. No one else ever could. That is the law of the universe.

*144*

From this day on, be determined that you will take charge of life and that you will realize all the God-given potential within you.

The greatest joy that anyone can ever discover is the joy of being yourself in God.

I want you to know—

BY GOD, YOU CAN DO IT.

## ABOUT THE AUTHOR

Robert G. Kirkley lives in Scotland, Maryland and is pastor of the Lexington Park United Methodist Church. Among his many interests are goose and duck breeding for conservation purposes. He has also been involved in efforts to ecologically reclaim the Chesapeake Bay.

In addition to his ministry, Dr. Kirkley lends his services as a chaplain to the Maryland State Police, providing counseling for policemen and their families.

*By God, You Can Do It* is Dr. Kirkley's first book.